Three Months with

REVELATION

Justo L. González

ABINGDON PRESS
Nashville

THREE MONTHS WITH REVELATION

Copyright © 2004 by Abingdon Press

Library of Congress Cataloging-in-Publication Data

González, Justo L.
  Three Months with Revelation / Justo L. González.
    p. cm.—(Three months)
  ISBN 0-687-08868-2 (alk. paper)
  1. Bible. N.T. Revelation—Study and teaching.   I. Title.   II. Series.
BS 2825.55.G66 2004
228'.0071—dc22

04 05 06 07 08 09 10 11 12 13 – 10 9 8 7 6 5 4 3 2 1

MANUFACTURED IN THE UNITED STATES OF AMERICA

C O N T E N T S

INTRODUCTION

General Introduction

This book is an invitation to study and to adventure. As a study it will require discipline. As an adventure, it will offer new panoramas and exciting challenges.

Let us address discipline. Every important goal in life requires a discipline. If a young person wishes to become, for instance, a doctor or a lawyer, it will be necessary to follow from an early age a discipline of study and learning. If we are concerned about our physical health, we try to follow a discipline of exercise and nutrition. Athletes who prepare to compete in the Olympics must subject themselves to a rigid discipline for years on end. And yet, when it comes to spiritual life, very few Christians are willing to subject themselves to a discipline that will develop and strengthen it. With the excuse that we should "pray without ceasing," we do not set aside a particular time for prayer. And, since the Bible is always there, ready to be opened and read whenever we need it, we do not set a program of study. The result is that both our prayer and our knowledge of the Bible suffer, just as the body suffers when instead of following an ordered diet and a discipline of exercise we eat whatever strikes our fancy and exercise only when we feel like it.

The first thing that we need in order to develop a discipline of study is to set aside a time and a place. The studies in this book follow a weekly rhythm: Each week there will be six short studies and a longer one. If you then follow this study privately, you will require at least half an hour a day for the six short studies and an hour for the longer one. Consider your weekly calendar and decide what the best time for you to set aside for study.

Once you have done this, make every possible effort to fulfill that commitment. Little by little, just as it happens with physical exercise, that study rhythm will become more and more important for you, and the time will come when, if for some reason you are not able to follow it, you will feel its need.

If you are using this book as part of a Bible study group that meets once a week, establish your rhythm of study so that the six shorter sessions take place on the days that you study in private, and the longer one on the day on which the group meets.

On the other hand, don't be too idealistic regarding the time you have set aside for study. Life always has its unexpected interruptions, and therefore very few people are able to follow a discipline of study without interruption. Sooner or later the day will come when it will be impossible for you to study during the time that you have set aside. In that case, do not be disheartened. That very day, even if at another time, try to study the material assigned for it.

A place is almost as important as a time. To the extent possible, have a particular place where you normally do your private study. This will help you avoid distractions. It will also be a convenient place for you to keep your Bible, this book, your notebook of personal reflections, and any other material that you may find useful.

The next important point in developing a discipline of Bible study is the method one follows. There are many good methods for the study of Scripture. The one that we shall follow in this book consists of three fundamental steps: **See, Judge,** and **Act.** However, before we discuss these three steps, there are two important elements that must be stressed, without which no Bible study can be productive: prayer and reflection.

At the very moment you begin each study, approach God in prayer. Ask that the Holy Spirit be with you during this study, helping you understand God's Word, and that the Spirit remain with you after you have completed the session, helping you follow what you have decided. Always remember that, even though you seem to be by yourself, you are not alone; God is right there with you. It is not just a matter of you and your Bible, but rather of you, your Bible, and the Holy Spirit—all of this linking you with the church, the body of Christ.

After a few minutes of prayer, devote some time to reflection, reviewing what you have studied before. In particular, remember those decisions you have made in previous days. Read your notebook. Evaluate what you have accomplished. Ask God for the strength to go forward.

Move then to the three steps of **seeing, judging,** and **acting**. As you will note, the material offered under each study is organized according to those three steps. The first, **seeing,** consists in examining the situation before you. In the case of these Bible studies, **seeing** will be examining the passage itself. What does it say? Why does it say it? Who are the main characters? What role do they play in the text? What is the context of what is said? In this first stage, we are not asking what the text might mean for ourselves or what it requires of us. We are only trying to understand the passage itself.

The second step, **judging,** consists in asking ourselves what the text might mean for us. Here, our personal experiences and our concrete situation become very important. We read the Bible in the light of those experiences and that situation, and ask what the Bible says about them. Therefore, when this book invites you to **judge,** it does not mean for us to judge the biblical text, but rather to invite the text to help us judge our own lives, situations, opportunities, and responsibilities. What does the text tell us about the church, about our faith, about our society? How does it affirm and support what we are doing and what we are? How does it question or correct it? What does the text call us to do or to be?

These first two steps lead to the third: **acting.** What we have seen in the biblical text, and the manner in which we judge that text refers to our reality, requires that we act in a specific way. We study the Bible not out of curiosity, but rather to be more obedient to God's will. Therefore, the process is incomplete if we are content with seeing and judging. If we are to be obedient, we must act.

Acting can take many diverse forms, which depend both on the text and on our own situation. For instance, the study of a certain passage may lead us to greater commitment to the poor and the needy in our community. The study of another passage may call us to witness to our fellow workers. And a third passage may call us to greater faithfulness in our participation in Christian worship. Furthermore, **acting** does not always imply physical activity. In some cases, acting may consist in a further prayer of repentance. In other cases, it may be abandoning a prejudice we have. Sometimes the action to be taken may be concrete and brief, for instance, calling someone whom we may have offended. In other cases, it may be a long-term decision, for instance, taking up a different career. But what is always true is that, if we really study the Bible in a spirit of obedience, the Word that comes from God's mouth will not return empty, but will accomplish that for which it was sent (Isaiah 55:11).

It is important to remember that we read and study the Bible not only to be *informed*, but also and above all to be *formed*. We do not read the Bible so much to learn something, as we read it to allow that something to shape our lives. Once again, the example of physical exercise fits the case. Whoever exercises, lifts weights not only to see how much she or he can lift (in order to be *informed*), but also, above all, to become stronger, to be able to lift greater weight (that is, to be *formed*). Likewise, our purpose in these Bible studies should be not only to learn something, to know the Bible better, but also to allow the Bible to shape us, to make us more in accord with the will of our Creator.

This implies that the method of **seeing, judging,** and **acting** should be more like a circle than like a straight line. What this means is that **acting** improves our **seeing,** so that in fact the method could be described as **seeing, judging, acting, seeing, judging, acting,** and so forth.

Every Bible study that we complete, each action that we take, will make us better able to move on to the next study. In order to understand this, think about a traveler in a valley. In that valley, the traveler **sees** a dense forest, a road that climbs a hill, and the position of the sun. On the basis of what he **sees,** the traveler

judges that he is not to try crossing the forest, but to try following the road. He also **judges,** on the basis of the position of the sun, in which direction he should go. Then he **acts**; he begins walking. Eventually he finds himself atop the hill, where he **sees** new views that allow him to **judge** the direction to be followed and that invite him to **act** in a way that he could not have guessed when he was in the valley. Therefore, his **acting** took him to a new way of **seeing.** The same will be true in a Bible study. If we make progress, we shall see ever wider views, and therefore not only will our **seeing** and **judging** lead us to a more faithful **acting,** but also our **acting** will clarify our **seeing** and **judging.**

What resources will you need to follow these studies? First of all, the Bible itself. Sometimes you will be tempted to shorten the time of study by not reading the Bible and reading only what this book says. The temptation will be even greater when the biblical passage is well known. It is important to resist that temptation. The purpose of this book is to help you in your study of the Bible, not to be a substitute for it. In the studies that follow, the Bible is quoted according to the New Revised Standard Version (NRSV). Therefore, if you use that version it will be easier to follow these studies. Naturally, if you have more time, you may wish to compare different versions in order to enrich your study. Some people following these studies have reported that they have used a Bible with large letters and wide margins, so that they could write notes and comments. That is up to you.

Second, use this book. Try to follow the rhythm of studies suggested, reading and studying each passage on the day assigned. We are too used to living life in a hurry. Instead of cooking a roast for five hours, we place it in the microwave for thirty minutes. Sometimes we want to do the same with our spiritual life. If it is good for us to do one of these Bible studies a day, why not go ahead and do them all at once? Here once again the example of physical exercise may be useful. If you try to do a month's worth of exercise in a single day, the results will be very different than if you establish a rhythm of exercise and stick to it.

Likewise, if we wish the Bible to shape us, to strengthen and to nourish our spiritual life, it is necessary for us to establish a rhythm that we can continue in the long run.

Third, you will need a notebook in which to write down your reflections, resolutions, and experiences. Write in it, not only what is suggested in some of the studies in this book, but also anything that seems relevant to you. If something strikes your interest, but you cannot follow up on it at the time, make a note of it. Write your answers to the questions posed in the book. Make a note of your decisions, your doubts, your achievements, your failures. Use it at the beginning of each study session, in the period set aside for reflection, in order to help you remember what you have learned and thought in the course of your three months' study of the book of Revelation.

Make sure that every time you begin a study session you have at hand all of these resources: your Bible, this book, your notebook, and a pencil or pen.

No other resources are absolutely necessary for these studies. But if you wish to study the book of Revelation more deeply, there are other tools that you may find useful: (1) several versions of the Bible, in case you want to compare them; (2) a good commentary on Revelation; (3) a dictionary of the Bible; (4) a biblical atlas. These resources will be particularly helpful if the seventh session of each week will be a group study and you are responsible for leading the group.

Finally, do not forget two resources readily available to you that are absolutely indispensable for any good Bible study. The first is your own experience. Some of us have been told that when we study the Bible we should leave aside all our other concerns. Nothing could be further from the truth. The Bible is here to respond to our concerns, and therefore our experience and our situation in life help us understand the Bible and hear God's Word for us today.

The second such resource is the community of faith. I have already pointed out that when you study the Bible you are not alone with your Bible; but the Holy Spirit of God is also there. Now I must add that, in a very real sense, your faith community is also there. The book of Revelation was probably written to be read out loud, in the gathering of the church. Therefore, when you read it, even though you may be alone, keep in mind the community of faith that surrounds and upholds you. Read it not only as God's Word for you, but also as God's Word for the church. That is why this book includes the longer Bible study each week: to encourage readers to use it in study groups. These groups may gather once a week, but during the other six days you will each know that the rest of the group is studying the same Bible passage.

I said at the beginning of this introduction that this book is an invitation both to study and to adventure. On this last point, it is best to say no more. Adventures are best when they are unexpected and surprising. Plunge then into the study of the book of Revelation, knowing that at some point it will surprise you, but knowing and trusting also that, even in such surprises, God is already there ahead of you, waiting for you with open arms!

A Word on Revelation

In other books in this series, I have not offered a specific introduction to the book of the Bible being studied. I have simply thought it best to allow readers to be introduced to the book by the very process of reading and studying it. Thus, for instance, in *Three Months with Matthew* we simply plunged into the study of Matthew without a word about its date of composition, author, purpose, or any other such matter.

However, the case of Revelation presents special circumstances. There are many wrong impressions and interpretations of the book that must be undone if we are to understand it properly. These various interpretations, though widely different in their content, agree on a fundamental point: they all look at Revelation as a mysterious outline of the events that will take place at the end, and of the order of those events. Thus there are debates between "premillennial" and "postmillennial" interpretations; there are disagreements about when the "great tribulation" is to come, and what it is; there are different views and proposed dates for Armageddon, and so forth. All these interpretations read Revelation much as we read a TV guide whose purpose is to let us know what comes next, and how much longer we must wait for our favorite program.

But that is not the purpose of Revelation. (Remember that Jesus himself told his disciples that it is not for us to know such things. See Acts 1:7.) Revelation was written late in the first century, at a time when Christian churches, particularly those in the province of Asia, were going through a difficult time of social and economic pressure and even of persecution. As a result, John was exiled on the island of Patmos. His book is a word of comfort and encouragement for the churches in Asia, calling them to stand firm in the faith and reminding them that the final victory belongs to Jesus and his followers.

Suppose then that, as some suggest, the beast whose number is 666 is the European Common Market or the Pope or Saddam Hussein. If that were the case, how could such a message inspire and comfort those Christians in Asia, late in the first century? How could it be a word from God to them? Revelation is not a program book outlining the final events, but a message to the churches in Asia—and therefore to all churches. John is writing to them, not in order to describe events that will take place centuries later, but to let them know that the purposes of God will not be thwarted, and that those who now oppose them will be put down.

On the other hand, Revelation certainly does relate to the events of our day. This is true not just of Revelation, but of the entire Bible. The Bible does not have some sections or books that tell us about the past and others that tell us about today. The whole Bible is God's Word for us today—and for all times. The reason for this is that believers repeatedly find themselves facing challenges, difficulties, and opportunities that are similar to those of earlier times. Therefore, what God had to say to the churches in Asia in the first century will also have much to say to the churches in North America in the twenty-first century.

There are two factors that make Revelation more difficult to understand than almost any other book in Scripture. The first is that Revelation is loaded with references and allusions to other books of the Bible—at a rate of more than one such allusion per single verse! It was written for people who knew the Hebrew Scriptures quite well and who therefore would recognize and understand those allusions. Unfortunately, that is no longer the case for most of us. Therefore, much of the "mystery" of Revelation becomes clear if we read it in the light of the rest of Scripture.

The second factor that sometimes makes Revelation difficult to understand is the situation in which the churches in Asia found themselves. They were under pressure from the whole of society as well as from Roman imperial authorities. The book refers repeatedly to that society and those authorities; but it could not do this openly because that would have made things even more difficult for Christians were the book to fall in the wrong hands. Therefore, Revelation frequently refers to Rome and to other realities of the time in cryptic words such as "Babylon the great," the harlot drunk with the blood of the martyrs, or the beast that comes from the sea.

Even so, if we read Revelation leaving aside the notion that what we are reading is a program for the end time, the book is not so difficult to understand. There certainly are in it, as elsewhere in the Bible, certain phrases and passages that are more difficult than the rest. But, as we shall see in our study, the central message of the book is quite clear, and it is quite relevant for today, just as it was for those early churches in Asia where it was read for the first time.

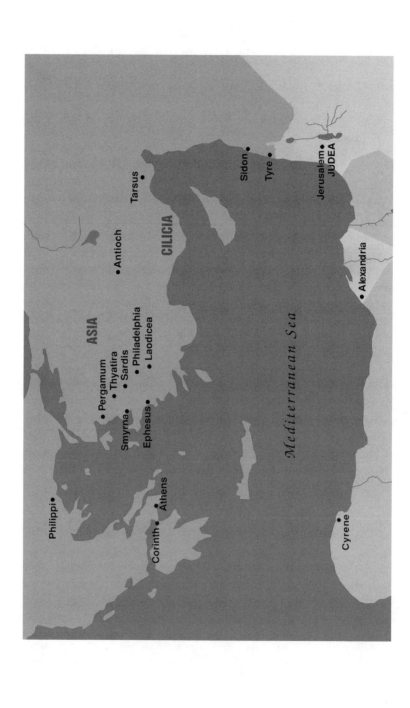

W E E K
ONE

First Day: Read Revelation 1:1-3

See: The book begins by saying that it is a "revelation" given to John. The Greek word for "revelation" is "apocalypse." That is why the book of Revelation is also called the Apocalypse of John. When we say that something is "apocalyptic" we often mean that it is disastrous or catastrophic, but that is not the original meaning of the word. In the sense of "revelation," Elijah's gentle whisper (1 Kings 19:12) is as "apocalyptic" as is this book that we begin to study today. The importance of this book is not really that it speaks of big events, of earthquakes, of showers of fire, and other such things, but rather that in this book God speaks to us. None other than God! When God speaks, that very fact, even when in the form of a gentle whisper, is greater and more worthy of admiration than the most disastrous earthquake. As the psalmist says, "he utters his voice, the earth melts" (Psalm 46:6). Later on (when studying Revelation 1:9) we will return to John himself, who received this revelation and wrote it. What he underscores here is that he does not claim to be the original author of what Revelation says, but claims only to give testimony of the revelation that has come to him from God by means of Jesus Christ (verse 1).

Notice also that in verse 3 there is a word of blessing on "the one who reads" and "those who hear." The book was written to be read aloud in the churches, just as Paul's letters were also read. It is for that reason that John speaks of a single person who reads and many who hear. In a certain way, the whole book of Revelation is a long letter written by John, at God's command, from the island of Patmos (with which we shall deal when studying verse 9), to the churches of the Roman province of Asia (verse 4). Notice also that hearing does not suffice. The blessing is for "those who hear and who keep what is written." In other words, it is for those who listen and obey. As we will see repeatedly in our study, those who do not obey in spite of having the opportunity to listen will reap judgment and destruction.

Judge: Place yourself in the situation of the churches to whom John addresses his letter. Remember that they were very small churches amid one of the mightiest empires that history had ever known. Conflicts had already emerged between the Christian faith and the imperial authorities, and soon such conflicts would lead to bloody persecutions. And the conflict was not only with political authorities, but in large measure also with the whole social order. When Christians refused to participate in idolatry, that very action closed many economic and social doors to them. Now their leader John was exiled on the island of Patmos. Patmos was near, but still inaccessible to them. When receiving the news that John's message had arrived, and that it would be read in church, people would go with joy and expectation, knowing that it would be a word of comfort.

Think now of all that you have heard about Revelation. According to the most common reading, it is a mysterious book that engenders panic. But how could such a book be a word of consolation for the suffering and perplexed believers of the first century, when John sent them this book? According to what many today seem to believe, Revelation is a sort of program that describes step-by-step the events of the end of the world (events that are happening right now according to some). But, how could such a book be of help to those Christians who first read and heard it, besieged as they were by hostile circumstances? Could it be that we have learned to read Revelation in the wrong way? Could it be that, instead of a book of fear, it is a book of hope? Could it be that, instead of a sad book, it is a book of comfort? Could it be that, instead of a sort of divine puzzle that it is necessary to decipher in order to discover what will happen at the end times, what we have here is a call to obedience here and now?

Act: Ask God to help you read this book as if you had never heard of it before; to listen to it with the same freshness and astonishment with which those first listeners in Ephesus, Laodicea, and the other cities of Asia must have heard what was being read. Do not try to read this book as if it were a puzzle or a crossword to solve. Read it rather as a word from God for you and for today's church. Pray that, as this book was a word of comfort and guidance for those first listeners, it will also provide you with comfort and guidance.

Second Day: Read Revelation 1:4-6

See: The book is addressed "to the seven churches that are in Asia." What was then called "Asia" was a relatively small Roman province in the western end of what today is Turkey. (See map on p. 14). Most likely, there were more than seven churches in Asia. John writes to these seven maybe in part because it was with them that he had more contact, but also because the number seven in the Bible is often used in the sense of perfection or entirety. Those "seven churches" are the seven that are mentioned by name, as we will see later on; but they also represent the whole church. The book is addressed to the seven churches, but also, by extension, to all of us.

The "seven spirits" can be interpreted in various ways. The most likely is that once again the number seven refers to the entirety, and that therefore those "seven spirits" are simply the wholeness of the Spirit of God, present in the church as a whole. (The phrase is used in this manner in other literature of the time.)

Notice that, as was customary in a letter, the book begins by saying who writes it (John) and to whom it is addressed (the seven churches). And immediately follows a greeting, as was also customary: "Grace to you and peace." You may wish to compare this with any of Paul's epistles, where you will see the same structure.

The greeting is very positive, for it includes only positive words: "grace, peace, faithful witness, loves us, he freed us, made us to be a kingdom, priests serving his God." Thus, from its very beginning, Revelation is a book not of fear, but of hope amid a situation that could seem overwhelming.

Judge: Imagine that you are in a situation like that of those early Christians who first heard the reading of this letter. The country (in this case the Roman Empire) is under the rule of an emperor who claims to be a god, and who therefore demands that all worship him. Over against such claims, John says that Jesus is "the ruler of the kings of the earth." That is to say that Jesus Christ is above the emperor, even if the emperor does not know or acknowledge it.

To ingratiate themselves with the authorities, there are people who give false witness against Christian believers, saying of them what those authorities wish to hear. Over against such false witnesses, John affirms that Jesus Christ is "the faithful witness." His testimony in favor of believers before the throne of God will be absolutely trustworthy.

Possibly already some members of the church have died as a result of conflicts with the state and society. Others fear that they also may die in such conflicts. Over against this fear, John declares that Jesus Christ is "the first-born of the dead," that is to say, the beginning of the resurrection that will also come to those who follow him.

Christians were then just a few people, and people of low status at that—slaves, laborers, fishmongers, and other salespeople in the markets. When they faced the surrounding society, they were before powerful magistrates, noblemen of the Roman Empire, priests of famous temples such as the one of Artemis in Ephesus. In the eyes of society, Christians were nobodies. But in contrast to this, John tells them that Jesus Christ has made them "a kingdom, priests serving his God." They have a dignity high above anything they could envy in magistrates, senators, nabobs, or representatives of the official religion.

Many Christians today find themselves in similar situations, "states maybe" not to the same degree—at least, not in the United States—but in many parts of the world there is serious persecution. I work among Hispanic Christians in the United

States, for instance, and what I meet are mostly poor people, some without legal documents, many with scant education, with a high level of unemployment, and with countless social, political, and economic difficulties. Yet it is mostly among such people that churches have grown.

Even those of us who belong to the "middle class" and to "mainline" denominations, when we compare our resources and those of the church to the resources of the mass media and to the resources that are used to promote vice and violence, we find that, like our ancestors in the faith, we are not very powerful. Most of us, like them, are nobodies.

But the text tells us that we are more than somebody. We are "a kingdom of priests serving God." We have a dignity and a value that nothing and nobody can take away from us—be it unemployment, poverty, lack of education, or even lack of immigration papers. Furthermore, with us is "the faithful witness, the first-born of the dead." We can rely on a power that is greater than any television network, any politician, or the richest merchant. We are kings and queens, priests and priestesses of the faithful witness and the first-born from among the dead. Let us not forget it.

Act: Go and look at yourself on a mirror. Tell yourself, if possible out loud: "I am a servant of Jesus Christ, and therefore a member of God's royal family. Nothing and nobody can take that away. From now on, I will behave as such." Repeat it until you actually imagine yourself with a crown. Throughout the rest of the day, when you face difficulties or when you feel that something or somebody minimizes or patronizes you or denies your dignity, remember what you saw in the mirror.

Decide to look at other people in the same way. Remember that you are not only royal, but also priestly. When you are tempted to minimize or to patronize somebody (especially a sister or brother in the church), remember that that person has also been called to reign with Jesus Christ. Look at others too as if they were wearing a crown, and show them due respect.

Third Day: Read Revelation 1:7-8

See: It is here that we find for the first time in Revelation a topic that will appear repeatedly in the book: the return of the Lord. Notice that what the text stresses is not so much the time of that return as the fact that it will be a vindication for those who believed in him, and a reproach for their enemies. The vindication is total. John tells us that "those who pierced him"—that is to say, his worst enemies, those who delivered him to death—will see him. And not only they, but "all the tribes of the earth" will wail—whether for themselves or for the sufferings of Jesus and his followers is not clear. What all this means is that, although at the moment the Christian faith is only that of only a handful of people who hardly count in Roman society, that faith will be vindicated, and even those who most tenaciously opposed it will have to acknowledge the lordship of Jesus Christ.

This is the meaning of the claims made by the Lord in verse 8: "I am the Alpha and the Omega" ("the beginning and the end"). In the Greek alphabet, the first letter was alpha, and the last was omega. Therefore "the Alpha and the Omega" is similar to what we mean today when we say "from A to Z." He is the Word that was before all things, and he will also have the last word, when all things have passed away.

On the other hand, to say that the Lord is the Alpha or the beginning or the one who was, is to say that he has been there from the beginning, although it is only recently, in his incarnation, that people have come to know him as Jesus. It means that his work is not only redemption, but also creation. As Alpha and beginning of all things, it is he who made all things, and therefore nothing is alien to him—not the church nor the Empire nor those who believe in him nor even those who do not believe. Ultimately all are his creatures, and all are subject to his power.

Judge: In difficult times, believers have to be careful not to think that only the church and its members belong to Jesus Christ. It is true that there is much wickedness in the creation, and the Bible speaks of it. But even so, this earth on which we live, as well as the sky that surrounds us, and even people who reject us or per-secute us, are still creatures of the same God. Although they do not know it, their Alpha and their beginning is none other than this Jesus Christ who is "the Alpha and the Omega," the begin-ning and the end, the one "who was and who is and who is to come." To think otherwise is to limit the power of Jesus Christ.

When you find opposition or inattention to the church and its message, are you sometimes inclined to think that Jesus is Lord of the church and of the faithful, but not of the rest of creation? That temptation is very normal when the church is besieged by the society around it, or when it feels that society simply doesn't pay much attention. Certainly, this must have been a temptation for the people to whom John addressed this book, and that is why he begins by stressing that Jesus Christ is not only the Omega, the one who in the end will come to judge the living and the dead, but also the Alpha, the beginning and the principle by which all things were created, and that it still sustains them.

This is important, because if we think that the rest of creation has nothing to do with our faith or with our Lord, we are limit-ing the scope of our faith and limiting the power of Jesus, who is "the Alpha and the Omega," the beginning and the end, the one "who is and who was and who is to come."

Act: Pray: Help me, Lord, to trust you and your power even in those places and situations where it seems that your power does not reach. Help me trust in your power in the church when I am among those who believe in you. And help me trust in your power outside of the church when I am among those who do not know you, or even reject and despise you. Make me remem-ber continually that you are the Alpha and the Omega, the beginning and the end, even until the end of time, when we shall see you face-to-face. Amen.

Fourth Day: Read Revelation 1:9-11

See: The name of John, the author of the book, appears here for a third time. For many reasons, it is not likely that this John is the same as Jesus' disciple by that name nor the author of the Fourth Gospel. He was, however, an important leader in the ancient church, for there are several documents of the time that refer to him as the main Christian teacher in Ephesus and its surroundings—that is to say, in the province of Asia. No matter what his connection with the original disciples, this John was a person of great authority in the churches to which he writes.

Given John's authority, it is important to note that he does not write as a superior to his subalterns, nor as a teacher to his followers, but rather as "your brother who share[s] with you." And this sharing is in three things: "the persecution and the kingdom and the patient endurance." This trio is interesting, because the persecution is present; the kingdom is future, or at least for the present it is hidden; and the patience is what allows John and the churches of Asia to live amid the present persecution and tribulation as those who await the kingdom.

John is on Patmos, a small island facing the coast of Asia Minor. Today Asia Minor belongs to Turkey, and Patmos to Greece. But from the island one can see the mainland. John is in exile there because of his faith, and in the distance, just beyond the horizon, is the land of his beloved churches.

John says that he was "in the Spirit," and that it was "on the Lord's day" that he received his revelation. From very early times, Christians began calling the first day of the week "the day of the Lord," because that was the day of the Lord's resurrection. John was now absent from his churches, exiled on the island of Patmos "because of the word of God and the testimony of Jesus." But the very day when his brothers and sisters beyond the sea gathered to adore, he had the vision that he writes about. He had this vision "in the Spirit," that is to say, in ecstasy. The voice that he hears on that occasion is the voice of Jesus, the same one whom he has just called the Alpha and the Omega and who now orders him to write what he sees.

Judge: Much is said in today's churches about the need to find leaders. The result is that much too frequently there are "leaders" who in fact are tyrants or people with dreams of greatness. Such supposed leaders appeal to many causes and reasons so that they are granted the respect and the authority they think they deserve: their commitment to the church, their age, how much they contribute with their offerings, their studies, the positions they hold in the church, and so forth. But examine what John says about himself, and you will see that his authority is based on two things.

John's authority is based in the first place in that he shares with the rest of the church both its difficulties and its hope for the kingdom. John has the authority to speak to the brothers and sisters of the seven churches and to offer them guidance amid their difficulties, because he himself has been and continues being part of that suffering body. If he is far from them, in Patmos, he owes this to the same difficulties and persecution that threaten them. To be a leader in the church it is necessary above all to be part of the church. It is necessary to participate in the hopes and the pains of the church as a whole. You cannot be a true leader from outside or from above. (Remember that, as an example of this, Jesus himself did not speak to us from a cloud, but rather was made flesh and dwelt among us, taking the human condition with all its pains, even unto death.)

You possibly have a position of leadership in your church. If you do, have you allowed that position to place you above other people? Or have you rather made use of that position to bring you closer to other people and to share more deeply in their struggles and joys?

Second, John's authority as a leader is based on the message that Jesus Christ has given him. It is not a message that he has invented. What is more, several times in the course of this book we will see that he himself does not understand all that he reports. It is a message that has been given to him by Jesus Christ, "the ruler of the kings of the earth," and therefore John cannot remain silent.

Through your biblical studies and your daily devotions, it is very possible that the Lord has given you a message for the rest of the church. It does not have to be a surprising message nor a vision like John's. But it is a message of what God wants us to do and to be as God's faithful people.

- Are you sharing with other people what you have learned?
- Are you helping them discover the will of God for them, as your own study of Scripture is helping you?
- Are you willing to hear what others—particularly others who are following these studies—have to say?

Act: Think of someone in your church who is going through particularly difficult times. Ask yourself what you can do to share in that person's pain and difficulties. Do it. Ask yourself what word the Lord may have for such a person. Pray over it. Review what you have studied and learned through these studies. When you reach the conviction that the Lord has given you a word for that person, go and communicate it, without boasting and without claiming that you have some special gift, but simply as a brother or sister in Christ.

Fifth Day: Read Revelation 1:12-16

See: At the end of the passage we studied yesterday, John had heard a voice ordering him to write. Now he sees again the one who speaks to him, and what he describes is a vision of Jesus Christ. The seven lampstands probably refer to the seven churches that the voice has just mentioned (verse 11) and that in turn represent the church as a whole. Jesus is amid the seven lampstands—that is to say, he is not far from the church, but in its midst. Later on John will have visions of what takes place in heaven. But here he speaks of what happens on earth, where the seven churches have to live, and where they have to face serious sufferings and temptations. And the most important thing, the first thing that John says, is that Jesus is in the midst of those churches, even when the eyes of the flesh can see little beyond sufferings and temptations.

John describes a powerful Jesus. His long vestments and belt of gold are symbols of royalty. His white hair is a sign of advanced age and therefore of wisdom. His eyes "like a flame of fire" indicate that he sees everything, even in the apparently darkest places. His feet "like burnished bronze" indicate stability, and his potent voice is a sign of authority. The two-edged sword is a common image that describes the Word of God that comes from his mouth. And his face radiant as the sun tells us that his glory is such that nobody can look directly upon it.

Judge: Here we are presented a vision of Jesus as powerful, and yet near to his church. Some people believe in a very powerful, but distant and inaccessible Jesus;. others, in a very loving, near, and affectionate, but weak Jesus. What is your Jesus like? How is Jesus preached and portrayed in your church? Is he a Jesus with eyes like fire, whose voice is like the thunder of many waters, but who is distant and uninvolved in our daily problems? Or is he a Jesus who strolls among us, always with a soft voice and dreamy eyes? If our Jesus were like the Jesus of John's vision, with eyes like fire and thunderous voice, but at the same time walking with us along the paths of life, what would the result be? Would we have more power to face and resist the temptations and the difficulties threatening us?

Act: Write in your notebook your answers to these questions. Resolve to discuss them with other people in your church, including your pastor.

Sixth Day: Read Revelation 1:17-20

See: John's vision is so startling that he falls "as though dead" at Jesus' feet. Remember that the glory of God is such that no one can see it and live: (Exodus 33:20). But the Lord not only allows John to see him, but even touches him and tells him not to fear. This is not because the Lord is not as powerful as he seems. On the contrary, just as the Lord tells John not to fear, he also proclaims his glory and his victory, telling John that he is the first and the last, the one who lives in spite of having died; and he lives in such a way and with such power that he has the keys of Death and of Hades (or of hell).

In other words, the reason John should not fear is not that Jesus is not powerful and even overwhelming, but rather that this Lord, so powerful that even death obeys him, is with John. He approaches John and even touches him. It is precisely because the Lord is who he is that John should fear neither the Lord nor the false lords of the world who persecute the church and show contempt for Jesus and his followers.

Judge: Go back to what you wrote yesterday on your notebook. Think of some situation in which the church that you know seems to be besieged, attacked, or criticized by external forces. (It can be, for instance, that the membership of your church consists mostly of people of scarce resources, and other people reject them because they are poor and lack formal education. It can be that your church is trying to face some problem in the neighborhood, and finds opposition on the part of some sectors of the same neighborhood or beyond. It can be that your ethnic minority church shares facilities with another congregation of the dominant culture, and that the members of that other congregation criticize your customs, your zeal in worship, your evangelizing drive, or something else.)

In the situation of which you are thinking, does your church fear some people or powerful elements in society? (For example, if your church members are poor, do they fear the rich who criticize them? Or, if they share facilities with a congregation of the dominant culture, do they fear the criticism of those other people?)

In such cases, what would happen if we took John's vision seriously? Remember that his vision is of a Lord almighty, beginning and end of all things, with eyes like fire and a voice like thunder. But it is also a vision of a Lord who approaches John, touches him, and tells him not to be afraid. Is it possible to have such a Lord, and still cringe in fear before our enemies? And if we continue fearing, could it be that we have not captured the message of John's vision?

Act: Review in your mind the actions and decisions that you have made in recent times. Were some of them due to fear? In such a case, can and should you now attempt to correct that action or decision, in view of the Lord almighty who tells you not to fear? Write down your reflections, and act on them.

Now review the actions and decisions of your church in recent times. Were any of them the result of fear? In such a case, should the church now try to correct that action or decision, in view of the Lord almighty who tells us not to fear? Write down your reflections and share them with others. Pray that the church may be able to act differently when a similar situation presents itself.

Seventh Day: Read Revelation 2:1–3:22

See: The text assigned for today is quite long. In previous days we have been reading at a rate of two or three verses a day. Today we have to read two whole chapters. The reason is that today's study serves as an introduction to what we will study next week. Thus, what we have read today we shall read again, at a slower pace and more thoroughly, during the coming week.

What we now begin to study is the section of Revelation known as "the seven letters." Although, as we have seen, the whole of Revelation is like a long letter to be read in the churches, in these two chapters (2 and 3) there are seven letters, each one specifically addressed to one of the seven churches already mentioned in 1:11: Ephesus, Smyrna, Pergamum, Thyatira, Sardis, Philadelphia, and Laodicea.

These letters have several characteristics in common, but each one of them is different. Therefore, today we shall study those common characteristics, and next week we will look each day at one of the letters and study it more carefully.

The first thing that we notice when reading these seven letters is that they are addressed not literally to the churches, but to the "angel" of each one of them. There has been much discussion as to what or who these angels are. Some Bible specialists point out that in antiquity it was thought that every human group, every nation, every city, and every church had its own particular angel that cared for it and represented it before God, and that it is to such angels that the letters are addressed. The problem is that the letters speak to such "angels" as if they were responsible for all the good and the evil in their churches, sometimes to the point of condemning the actions and attitudes of such "angels." Other interpreters think that these "angels" are the pastors or leaders of each church. Such an interpretation also presents its difficulties. Still others think that the "angel" of each church is a symbolic figure that represents it, as when we say, for example, that the spirit of a church is very hospitable or that another church has a cantankerous spirit. In short, it is impossible to know exactly what or who these "angels" are to whom the letters are addressed.

It is much more important to note that in each one of these letters the one who speaks is not John but the Lord. The letters must be written by John; but they carry a message from the Lord. In each letter the Lord is described in a different way, sometimes using metaphors we have already seen in the way John describes his vision. As we shall see next week, in some cases one can see a relationship between what is said of the Lord (that is to say, how he is described) and the message to a specific church. In others, the connection is not all that clear.

Notice that in each letter, after that description of the Lord, there is a series of declarations about the life of that particular church. In some cases, all that is said is positive. In others, everything is negative. In most, something positive is said, but at the same time something negative is criticized.

Then follows an admonition that appears in every letter: "Let anyone who has an ear listen to what the Spirit is saying to the churches." Note that, although that admonition appears toward the end of each letter to a particular church, it refers to what the Spirit says "to the churches." This means that the specific message to each church must be heeded by all others, so that although the message is applied to a church in particular, in fact it is for the church as a whole. These letters never circulated independently of each other, for they were always part of a single book. Thus, when somebody in Ephesus, for instance, read the book, the church of Ephesus heard, not only the message directed specifically to it, but also the messages to the other six churches.

Finally, each letter includes a promise, although these promises vary: "To everyone who conquers, I will give. . . ."

Judge: You know several congregations, either in your own denomination or in others. Think of three or four of them. Imagine that the Lord wants to send a specific message to each one. What characteristic or actions of the Lord do you believe will be stressed in that message? (For instance, if it is a church in which people are always judging one another, possibly the Lord would say something like: "I am the one who forgives, the one who gave my life for the sins of others." Or if it is a church rent by divisions and gossip, possibly the Lord would say: "I am the one who calls to love and unity, the Lord of truth, and not of lies, neither of rumors.")

Act: Think now of your own church. What do you believe the message of the Lord to it would be? Remember that in most of the seven letters some good things are mentioned, as well as some that are not so good. For what do you think the Lord would praise your church? For what would God not praise it?

Write in your notebook a letter to your church, as similar as possible to the seven letters that we are studying, but referring specifically to the problems and achievements of your church. Pray over what you have written. Ask the Lord to help you find the proper means to share your concerns in a positive and constructive way.

For Group Study

If this seventh study of the week is a group study, the person directing it can request participants to write letters as suggested above. This can be done in groups of three or four participants. Then share what each group has written.

Another way of doing this could be to describe a different church for each group to think about (without mentioning specific names of churches). For example, direct a group to think of a church whose problem is lack of evangelizing zeal, another to think of a church that is divided because some like the pastor and others do not; another group could consider a church with much enthusiasm but lacking in economic resources; and so on. Toward the end of the session, ask each group to read its letter out loud and to explain why they have chosen to write as they did.

If time permits, begin a discussion on what sort of letter the Lord would write to your congregation.

W E E K
TWO

First Day: Read Revelation 2:1-7

See: At the beginning of each study during this week, look up on the map the name of the city to which the letter you are studying is addressed. In today's study that city is Ephesus. This was the most important of the seven cities to which John addresses his letters. It was a seaport through which many of the goods produced in the other cities were shipped (except for goods from Smyrna, which was also a seaport). Today the city is several miles away from the sea, because the silt of the river that flowed by Ephesus has extended the dry land.

Chief among the glories of Ephesus was the great temple to Artemis or Diana, one of the seven marvels of the ancient world. All that now remains standing of that great structure is a single column. The city had a beautiful theater whose ruins still stand. (In Acts 19 there is an episode in which both the temple of Artemis and the theater played an important role. If time allows, you may wish to read in Acts about the origins of the church in Ephesus.)

In his words to the church of Ephesus, the Lord describes himself as "him who holds the seven stars in his right hand, who walks among the seven golden lampstands." Here the Lord is saying that all the churches, even that of Ephesus, are in his hands, and that he walks amid them. This is a sort of warning, so that the church in Ephesus will take what follows seriously.

When reading this letter to the Ephesians, we see that this church had some good traits. Most important, it knew how to distinguish between true and false teachers. The letter praises them for not allowing themselves to be deceived by "evildoers" or by false apostles. Nor have they accepted the teachings of the

"Nicolaitans." For the time being, it is not important that we know exactly to what each one of these sentences refers. The main point is that the Ephesians seem to have been zealous believers, upholding true doctrine. They are also praised for their patience and for their works.

But not everything is rosy. The Lord tells the Ephesians that he has something against them: that they have "abandoned the love you had at first." Apparently, and perhaps as a result of their zeal for truth and correct doctrine, the Ephesians no longer loved one another as they did earlier. And the Lord is not pleased over it. On the contrary, in spite of all they do in defense of correct doctrine, and in spite of all their works and their patience, the Lord threatens to remove their lampstand from among the others—that is, to destroy them as a church.

Judge: To sacrifice love for the sake of doctrine is always a temptation in the life of the church. What happened to the church of Ephesus happened again, and even worse, to the medieval church when it decided to establish the Inquisition in order to protect the purity of its doctrine.

Do you think that it is possible to work for the purity of doctrine without falling into the trap of lacking in love or compassion? Think of the various Christian denominations in your own community. Do they attack and criticize each other over questions of slight importance, in such a way that the witness of all suffers? Do you believe we should leave those matters of lesser importance to the opinion of each one, or of each denomination, and center our attention on the love that is the very foundation of the Christian life?

On the other hand, it is true that the church must make sure that its teachings (and those of its teachers) are correct. When somebody teaches false doctrine, that person must be corrected, called to account, and others must be warned about whatever error is being taught.

What do you do when you decide that somebody is in error? Do you pray for that person? Do you speak to that person with love and patience? Do you pray for him or her?

Act: Pray: Lord, help me and help my church to distinguish between correct and false doctrine. But help us do this without losing the love that must be at the center of our faith. Help us love even those people with whom we most differ. Help us conquer in love, so that at the end, as to conquerors, you may give us to eat of the tree of life. Amen.

Second Day: Read Revelation 2:8-11

See: The second church addressed is in Smyrna. On the map you will note that Smyrna, like Ephesus, was also a seaport, about fifty kilometers north of Ephesus. Of all the seven cities in this section of Revelation, Smyrna is the only one that is still a sizable city (the Turkish city of Izmir). In the time of John, it was the second largest city in the province of Asia, after Ephesus. It was a city proud of its history. It had been destroyed by an earthquake about seven hundred years earlier, and it had been reborn from its own ruins. It was a center for emperor worship, and it was proud of its loyalty to Rome.

Apparently there were in Smyrna serious conflicts between Christians and some Jews. Possibly those whom John calls false Jews were in fact "judaizers," that is to say, Christians of Gentile origin who insisted on following the laws of Moses and living as Jews. John and most of the readers to whom he addresses this book were Jews by birth who now had embraced Christianity. This can be seen in the very frequent use of allusions to the Old Testament, many of which would be understood only by those who had been raised and formed inside the tradition of Israel. (Remember that there is not a single verse in Revelation that does not contain an allusion to the Old Testament or to other Jewish literature of the time.) For them, Christianity was the fulfillment of the promises made to Israel, now accessible also to people of Gentile origin who believed—and this, without necessity of being circumcised or becoming Jews. Thus, for John and his readers, "false Jews" would include both people of Jewish origin who refused to accept Christianity and those of Gentile origin who insisted on becoming Jews in order to be truly

Christian. It is possibly to the latter that John refers as those "who say that they are Jews and are not, but are a synagogue of Satan."

Christians in Smyrna were in a precarious situation. Amid a fabulously rich city, Christians were generally poor. For that reason the message tells them "I know ... your poverty, even though you are rich." Social pressure and the threat of persecution were serious. The "ten days" of affliction may refer to a long time, but one that would come to an end, for the number ten frequently meant "many."

Since the situation in Smyrna was a matter of life or death, the letter to the church in that city insists on the theme of life and death. Jesus is described as the one "who was dead and came to life." The central exhortation of the letter is, "Be faithful until death, and I will give you the crown of life." And the promise at the end of the letter is that "whoever conquers will not be harmed by the second death."

Judge: Think of your own church. Is it in a rich or poor area? There are countries (and cities or regions) that are proud of their history, as if they were the best in the entire world. In such places, people sometimes resent the presence of "those who are different". That was true in Smyrna, where Christians seemed to be a threat to the glory of the city. In such countries and communities those who are poor are not well regarded, because they seem to be a stain on the prestige of the place. Have you ever felt that the poor are regarded with contempt where you live? Or have you ever been among those who dislike, resent, or exclude those who are poorer or less educated than they? In such cases, what is the significance of the words of Jesus, telling believers of Smyrna that, although they seem poor, they are in fact rich?

In your own congregation, are most members rich or poor? What place do they occupy in the social scale of the whole city where the church is located? Would Jesus tell them, as he tolds-the Smyrneans, that, although they seem to be poor they are in fact rich?

There are places in the world where believers are oppressed and persecuted, because they are thought to be a subversive element in society. They are different from the rest of the society, and since they do not fit, it seems best to destroy them or at least to limit their freedom, so that they can do no harm. Do you know of places where the church is going through difficulties similar to those of that ancient church in Smyrna?

Act: Make an effort to learn more about the conditions in which believers in Jesus Christ live in different parts of the world, especially in those places where they are deemed subversive, or are accused of not adapting to the uses of the rest of society. If you do not know about such places, talk to your pastor, who may give you some leads. Study the church in that place and compare it with yours. Do believers living in such circumstances have something to teach us? Write down your reflections.

Third Day: Read Revelation 2:12-17

See: The third letter goes to the church in Pergamum, a city about seventy kilometers to the north of Smyrna. Although smaller than Ephesus or Smyrna, Pergamum was an important city from which the Roman Empire governed the province. That is probably the reason that the letter to Pergamum says that the church in that city dwells "where Satan's throne is." Due to its political importance, Pergamum was also a center of emperor worship. Also, there was a great temple to Zeus whose foundations, today in ruins, are still imposing.

Apparently the church in Pergamum had remained strong amid persecutions so violent that a believer named Antipas had died as a witness of Jesus Christ. For this the Lord praises it.

But, on the other hand, that church had not been as careful in sifting the various doctrines circulating among its members. Not much is known about the "Nicolaitans" to whom the text refers. They may be the same as the followers of "the teaching of Balaam," since in Greek *Nicholas* means "conqueror of the people," and in Hebrew Balaam has approximately the same meaning.

Tomorrow we shall deal with the doctrines of "Jezebel," which were possibly the same or at least very similar to those of the "Nicolatitans" and the "followers of Balaam." No matter what those teachings may have been, it is clear that according to Revelation they drew people away from the true God. This is probably what is meant by the reference to "fornication" in this letter. Most interpreters believe that what we have here is the use of an imagery common to the prophets of ancient Israel: those who go after other people's gods fornicate and commit adultery against the true God.

The "sharp two-edged sword" is an image that John has used before, when he told us that such a sword came out of the mouth of the Lord. In Greek there are two terms for "sword." The one that is used here does not refers not to the short and light sword that was used in battle, but to the heavier sword that an executioner employed. Such a sword was a symbol of the power of the empire and of the authority of its rulers. Thus, when it declares that Jesus has that sword, the letter is saying that power of life and death is his, and is not ultimately in the hands of the imperial authorities who for the time being persecute the church. And in warning Christians in Pergamum that if they do not get rid of false doctrine he will come and punish them with the same sword, he is reminding them that they should fear and respect his authority above that of secular rulers.

Judge: In our present situation, most of us do not have to face an openly hostile government. But we do have to face a culture that makes Christian obedience ever more difficult. This means that the firm commitment that was required of Christians in Pergamum is also required of us today.

Take an example. In our culture and society there are "gods" that it is necessary to obey in order to be accepted as normal members of society. One of these gods is money. We are constantly told, in a thousand different ways, that success in life consists of making money. The mass media offer us, as examples to emulate, not saintly people who offer their life to serve as a blessing to others, but those who make money in big business, the actors who receive fabulous sums to make a movie, or sports heroes whose salaries could feed thousands of hungry people. The pressure on us to emulate such people is enormous. And this is more so for the young, even in our churches. If one of the guises that Satan takes in our day is this twisted notion of the purpose of life, then we can say that, like those ancient believers in Pergamum, we live "where Satan's throne is."

In that case, who are those faithful witnesses after the fashion of Antipas whom we must put forth as examples for our youth and for the entire church? How have they resisted the powers of the world that claim that the purpose of life is something other than love and service?

Act: Make a list of those "faithful witnesses." Develop a plan or strategy to make their lives known, and to offer them as examples for others to emulate, in contrast with the heroes of the mass media. Discuss this with others in the church, so that they may help you in this task and find ways to present the lives and deeds of such people as an example to the young and to the entire community.

Fourth Day: Read Revelation 2:18-29

See: Up to this point the route that the messenger with the word to the seven churches would follow ran almost directly north, from Ephesus to Smyrna and then to Pergamum. Now the route turns southeast, to the city of Thyatira, some seventy kilometers from Pergamum. Thyatira was not as imposing nor as important as the three previous cities. It was a center of crafts and of small industry, mainly in metallurgy and the dyeing of cloth. Remember that in Acts 16:14 we are told that Lydia, the seller of purple, was from Thyatira. It is possibly because of the interest in that city for the practice of metallurgy that the text emphasizes that the Lord who sends the message is one "who has eyes like a flame of fire, and whose feet are like burnished bronze." The latter was an alloy of copper, tin, and zinc that was produced in places such as Thyatira.

Since in that time most crafts and small industry were organized around religious guilds devoted to the service of some god or goddess, quite often those who opted for the Christian faith had to pay a high economic price. If they refused to join in worshiping the god of their guild, they could not belong to the guild, and therefore they would not have a market for their products, or sources where they could buy the materials required for their work.

Apparently, that situation led some people in the church to try to look for arrangements or compromises that would allow believers to participate in such guilds and their religious activities without giving up their participation in church. In Thyatira, such was the position of a prophetess whose name is not known, but whom John calls "Jezebel." He gives her that name because Jezebel was the Canaanite who married king Ahab and led Israel to "whoredoms and sorceries" (2 Kings 9:22). As in that passage of the Old Testament, the "fornications" of Jezebel are not physical adultery, but rather the theological adultery of running after other gods instead of the one true God. And, as in the Old Testament, this Jezebel and her children (that is to say, those who follow her) will pay with their life.

All of this, however, does not mean that the church in Thyatira as a whole should be condemned. On the contrary, the Lord praises them for their love, faith, service, patience, and works—to such a point that their works have improved with time. Those who follow "Jezebel" seem to be only a minority that claims to be better informed than the rest. It is against them that the harsh words in the letter to Thyatira are addressed. For the rest of the church, there is commendation and words of encouragement.

Judge: What are some of the pressures that today, and in situations that you know, incite Christians to compromise their beliefs? Possibly these will not be as clear and drastic as those in ancient Thyatira; but even so, there may still be parallel cases. Let us see some.

As I write these lines, I have just talked on the phone with a friend who is an engineer. He had an excellent job with a company where he had been working for several years. One day he was assigned to a team whose task was to design guidance systems for rockets with atomic weapons. After much thought and prayer over the matter, and after discussing it with his church and family, he decided that he could not help design such devices. He requested to be assigned to another task. When his request was rejected, he simply resigned. He and his family spent several months in poverty while he sought other employment.

Another sister is a chemist, and she worked in a laboratory that had a contract with a tobacco company to analyze the nicotine and tar content in their products. The boss ordered her to falsify the results of her analyses, and she refused. From that point on, her position in the laboratory became more and more difficult until she was finally fired. She was unemployed for more than two years. During that time, she could not pay her mortgage and lost her home.

What do you think John would have said about those two cases? What do you think "Jezebel" would have said? What would you say?

Perhaps the most saddening fact about these two cases is that most brothers and sisters in the churches of these two people did not find ways to lend them support, and some even refused to try to understand the reasons for their actions. Could it be that they refused to understand because they were involved in similar compromises?

Act: Think about the two cases mentioned above. Have you ever found yourself in a similar situation, although maybe not as dramatic? What did you do? Who provided you with support and guidance? What would you do now, if the same situation presented itself again?

Think of your sisters and brothers in your church. Who among them have paid or are paying a high price for their faithfulness? How are you able to lend them support? Write down your answers and think of ways to support those people who are making sacrifices for their faith.

Fifth Day: Read Revelation 3:1-6

See: The road still leads southeast, and we now arrive at the city of Sardis, some fifty kilometers from Thyatira. Sardis was a walled city built in a place that apparently made it invulnerable. But in past centuries its enemies had conquered and destroyed it twice, both times entering the city surreptitiously, and then opening the doors to the invading army. Now, in John's time, it was famous because it produced a black wool of great value.

The Lord does not have much good to say about the church in Sardis. In contrast with Smyrna, where the church seemed poor but was rich, the church in Sardis seems to be alive when in fact it is dead. There is still in it some life, some few things that are about to die and that the church should affirm. But if it is not vigilant, the Lord will come to this church "like a thief"—that is to say, without warning and when he is least expected. This is a reference both to Jesus' parables about the necessity of being alert and to the previous history of Smyrna, conquered and destroyed twice by enemies who entered the city very much like thieves.

But not everything is lost. They are still in Sardis some "who have not soiled their clothes" and who will walk with the Lord in white garments. This is a double allusion. On the one hand, it would remind readers of their own baptism, for in the ancient church those who were baptized, when leaving the waters, were dressed in white robes as a sign of victory and of newness of life. On the other hand, it would remind believers in Sardis of the contrast with the black wool that had given fame to their city and that produced much of its income.

Judge: Do you know churches that, although they seem to be alive, are in fact dead or nearly so? Although in some circles people speak of a church as "alive" when its worship is lively, with much activity and even noise, that is not necessarily what determines how "live" a church is. Note that in the letters we have already studied, when churches are praised, not once is the form of their worship mentioned. What has been praised is love, faith, patience, steadfastness, and works of love.

The same sort of question that we ask about churches we may ask about ourselves. Are we truly alive in the faith? Here again the criteria are the same: love, faith, patience, and so forth.

Act: List the characteristics of a church or an individual that are alive in their faith (such as love, faith, and so on). Giving the matter some thought, choose the one (or the ones) in which you or your congregation are most deficient. Pray requesting God to strengthen you in that aspect. Consider ways to show that new strength. (For instance, if it is works of mercy that you lack, you may decide to volunteer for work in a shelter for the homeless.) Write down your reflections and your decisions.

Sixth Day: Read Revelation 3:7-13

See: The city of Philadelphia was about fifty kilometers to the southeast of Sardis. It had been founded some two hundred years earlier by a king of Pergamum who had named it "Philadelphia," that is to say, "fraternal love," in honor of his brother who had shown exceptional loyalty. But a great earthquake had totally destroyed it in the year 17, and when John wrote Revelation the city was still in the process of reconstructing some of its main buildings and temples.

Apparently, one of the main problems of the small church in Philadelphia was what we have already seen in Sardis and other places: the question of who were the true heirs to the promises made to Abraham and his descendants. Here, those "who say that they are Jews and are not" may be Jews who have refused to accept Jesus Christ or Christian judaizers of Gentile origin, who now insisted on obeying all the Jewish laws, as if they were better Jews than the Jews themselves. In any event, these "false Jews" set up rules that excluded the members of the church who did not agree with them. It is for that reason that the themes of the "key of David" and of open and closed doors play such an important role in the whole letter to Philadelphia. In Isaiah 22:22, the "key of the house of David" is a symbol of the authority given to those who control access to the king, and who use their power on his behalf. Therefore, whoever has the "key of David" controls access to God and to the messianic promises. If Christians in Philadelphia are now excluded by certain "false Jews," they should not worry too much about it, for it is not their enemies, but Jesus Christ, who has the true key and who has opened for them a door that nobody can close.

The reference in verse 12 to "a pillar in the temple" probably points to the custom, when a temple or another public building was built, of recording on some columns, or on the floor, the names of the main contributors to the project (much as today in some churches such names are placed on pews, windows, or hymnals). Since many temples in Philadelphia were in the process of reconstruction, the prominent and rich citizens could record their names on the columns by giving substantial contributions. Christians could not do the same, not only because they were poor, but even more because they would not contribute to the construction of pagan temples. But the Lord promises them something better: in the temple of God, such faithful believers will be as columns, and the names they will bear as an engraving will be nothing less than the name of God and of the new Jerusalem. This means that it is God who has put them there, and nobody will be able to remove them. (Although there is no record of a similar situation in Philadelphia, a case is known in Rome of a conflict between those who wanted to remove a column of a building and the descendants of the original donor.)

Judge: Almost all the seven letters contain some point of criticism, calling the church to greater faithfulness. The two exceptions are the letters to Smyrna and to Philadelphia. However, everything seems to indicate that, in human terms, these were two of the weakest churches among the seven. They were poor and were besieged not only by the government and by pagan society as a whole, but also by the "false Jews" to whom John refers.

When today we think of a strong church, on what grounds do we recognize one as such? If we imagine that the signs of a strong church are having many members, much money, and great influence, are we not using different criteria than the ones the Lord uses here? Could it be that many of the churches that seem to be weaker and in more precarious situations turn out to be the most faithful?

Act: Pray that, as in the case of Philadelphia, the difficulties facing your church may become the basis for greater fidelity and obedience. When praying, make a list of those things your church lacks (money, space, power, or whatever), and ask God, not necessarily to give your church those things, but rather to help it be a faithful church, either with such things, or without them.

Seventh Day: Read Revelation 3:14-22

See: The city of Laodicea, thirty kilometers southeast of Philadelphia, completes the wide circuit that John's messenger would have to make, taking John's book and the seven letters included in it. Militarily, it had never been a powerful city, because its setting made it more fit for trade than for war. Therefore, when the Roman Empire extended to the point of including the province of Asia, and brought with itself a period of relative peace in the region, Laodicea began to prosper. Already by the year 60 it was so rich that when an earthquake destroyed many of its buildings the city refused to accept the help of the imperial coffers, and insisted on rebuilding with its own resources. Its main industry was processing wool, from which workers in Laodicea produced high quality fabric. The city was also famous for a powder that, dissolved in water, was used as medicine for the eyes.

Near Laodicea, on a neighboring mountain, was the city of Hierapolis, whose springs of thermal waters were famous for their healing powers, and where the sick went in the hope of being healed. But the water that was hot and therefore healthy in Hierapolis was only lukewarm by the time it reached Laodicea, and the minerals it contained, though not enough to confer the water's healing power, were certainly enough to make it taste bad.

All this is in the background of what the Lord tells John to write to the church in that city. The warning, for instance, that the church in Laodicea is neither cold nor hot and that therefore the Lord will spit it out of his mouth (verses 15-16) would remind the Laodiceans of the bad reputation of their city's water, which was always lukewarm and which few considered truly drinkable. The same is true of the references to the nakedness and blindness of the Laodiceans, and of the call to that church to buy "white robes" and to anoint their eyes.

The words of the Lord to this church that feels rich and powerful are devastating. In fact it is "wretched, pitiable, poor, blind, and naked" (verse 17). In contrast with the other churches, about which the Lord says something good, all that is said here is negative.

Even the best-known and most often quoted part of this letter to the Laodiceans, while indeed a word of hope, is also a word of judgment. Verse 20 includes the words, "I am standing at the door, knocking." That has been the subject of famous paintings, usually depicting the willingness of Jesus to enter into the human heart. But in this context it implies a word of condemnation for the church of Laodicea. Jesus, the Lord of the church, is left out, standing at the door and knocking. While the church meets to celebrate the Lord's Supper, which was the center of Christian worship, Jesus, instead of being present in the Supper, is outside waiting to be admitted. In a way, the church itself has excluded him. It is for that reason that he is at the door calling—and the word that is used here refers not to the gentle knock of a visitor but to the hefty blow of an impatient master locked out of his own home. They have left him outside of his own house, and he knocks at the door, not as a guest waiting to be admitted, but with the imperious knock of the owner of the house. Those who do not open the door to him are not only deaf, but also rebels and usurpers.

Judge: Here we have a church of whose difficulties not a word is said. Apparently, the difficult situations that faced believers in Philadelphia or in Smyrna did not exist in Laodicea. Nothing is said of "false Jews" or of afflictions or of threats from the surrounding society. There is not even a dissident group with strange ideas, such as the "Nicolaitans" mentioned in other letters. On the contrary, everything seems to go well. The church of Laodicea, amid a rich and prosperous city, seems to have participated in that prosperity without much difficulty. And yet, this is the most scathing of the seven letters to the churches in the province of Asia. Could it be that the worst danger that threatens the church, much worse than persecution, criticism on the part of the rest of the society, or economic and theological difficulties, is an easy life, an abundance of goods, the lack of real challenges?

Think of the churches you know. Are there some that resemble the church of Laodicea, which had everything and yet lacked the most essential—a church where the lack of difficulties had weakened the very heart of faith, and which believed itself to be rich and powerful when in fact it was poor and wretched? Do you know of other churches like the one in Philadelphia, with many enemies and critics, and yet faithful to the Word of the Lord?

Review what you have learned about each one of the seven churches. Which of them does your own congregation most resemble? Why? Write down your reflections.

Ask the same question about your denomination as a whole. Is it respected and accepted by the rest of the society? Is there a danger that precisely for that reason your denomination may become like the church in Laodicea?

What do these seven letters teach us about the standards by which churches must measure their success?

Act: Share your reflections with other people in your church. Together, try to determine the message of these seven letters for your church. Which of the seven letters best applies to you? What must you do so that the promises at the end of each of those letters may be fulfilled in you? Carry these conversations into action as you and others make decisions about the life and programs of your church.

For Group Study

Try to place these seven letters in a global context. If possible, ask different members of the group to try to learn about the situation of the church in a particular country. Some, for instance, can study the current condition of the church in some of the countries of the former Soviet bloc. Others can study the condition of the church in some Latin American or Asian country—maybe their own country of origin. Each one should then think of the seven letters of Revelation and try to decide which of them applies best to the situation they have studied.

When the group meets, and after giving each one an opportunity to present the results of their study and meditation, ask the group to discuss which of the churches of Revelation yours most resembles. Conclude the session by asking what we must do to be more like the church of Philadelphia and less like those of Laodicea, Ephesus, or Sardis.

W E E K
THREE

First Day: Read Revelation 4:1-3

See: After the seven letters, the scene changes radically. Up to this point, John's vision has not taken him elsewhere. He has remained on the island of Patmos, where he sees the Lord, who then tells him what he is to write to each of the seven churches. Now the action takes place in heaven. Such changes in scenarios are one of the traits of Revelation that sometimes make it difficult to understand this book. The narrative in Revelation is not a linear action, in which events would follow one after the other in a strict chronological order. On the contrary, there is a double action, in which some things happen on earth and others happen in heaven, and the two levels of action are interrelated. It is as if we attended a play with a two-tiered stage. At each of the two levels there is a drama taking place. Most of the characters of the scene below do not know what is taking place above and therefore do not fully understand what happens on their own level.

John's visions are like a window through which characters on the terrestrial stage can see the celestial one, and thus achieve a more exact understanding of what is happening on earth. John ascends to heaven "in the Spirit,"—that is to say, that it is the Spirit of God who offers him a vision as if he were physically present in heaven. And the first thing he sees is a vision of God. Since among Jews one took care not to mention the name of God, John does not tell us directly that it was God. Through his book, even though he will speak of the "name of God," and of the "Spirit of God," he will usually refer to God through phrases such as the "one seated on the throne." Naturally, the description of the one sitting on the throne as "like jasper and carnelian" must not be taken as a literal description. What John is saying is that his glory was immense, brilliant, and blinding like precious stones. Likewise, the rainbow that looks like an emerald is an indication of the glory that surrounds God.

Judge: Do you think that for the persecuted Christians of the churches in Asia John's vision would be a word of comfort and affirmation? Imagine that an entire government and society try to make you fearful, and that they have enormous power. It is nothing less than the great Roman Empire, with all its pomp, its prestige, and its power that is threatening these believers. But now John tells them of a vision of the glory of God. It is such a grand vision that before it all the kings and thrones of the earth pale by comparison. Later on we shall see that the one who sits on the throne does keep watch over his persecuted and oppressed followers. Would John's vision not make believers more steadfast in their beliefs?

Think now of yourself and the pressures in your life. Those pressures sometimes seem overwhelming. Quite often, there is nothing we can do against them. Problems loom large. Resources are scarce. Sometimes it even seems that the whole world is against us. In such cases, we would do well to remember John's vision. There is One who is seated on the throne, before whom the greatest powers on earth pale. If we are faithful, this One is also faithful and will give us victory. What else do we need in order to continue the struggle in the certainty that, to those who conquer, he will give the crown of life?

Act: Make a list of the things you most fear. Write them down in a column on your notebook. One at a time, write next to each item: "But God is greater." Before moving to the next one, take some time to reflect on what that means in that particular case. Pray asking God to help you evaluate your problems, fears, and difficulties as they should be, taking them seriously, but always placing them under the overarching reality of God's love and power, so that you will not be overwhelmed.

Second Day: Read Revelation 4:4-5

See: Around God's throne, John sees twenty-four thrones, and seated on each throne is an elderly person dressed in white and wearing a golden crown. These twenty-four elders represent the twelve tribes of Israel and the twelve apostles. Throughout the Bible, the number twelve is a sign of something complete, and it is found repeatedly in Revelation with the same meaning. Here, what is meant is that next to God, surrounding the heavenly throne, the entire people of God also reigns—both the descendants of Abraham according to the flesh, the people of Israel, and Abraham's descendants by faith, the church. John himself was a Jew, and he saw in Christianity not the negation of the faith of Israel, but its culmination and fulfillment. The same God who chose Israel is the God who now has chosen the church.

These elders wear white robes. In antiquity the color white was a sign of victory. Thus, the elders represent the triumphant people of God. Remember that the promise of victory appears repeatedly in the seven letters.

The thrones and the crowns show that the faithful share the kingdom of God. Remember that John has already said that God's followers are "a kingdom of priests." Here we see the people of God enthroned around God. (But, as we shall see later on, the twenty-four elders do homage to God and are never even compared to the One who sits on the throne.)

The significance of the "four living creatures" will be discussed tomorrow, as we study the verses in which they are described.

Judge: We find John's imagery imposing: thunder and lightning, winged beings, a glassy sea. But in fact the most imposing aspect of John's vision is its scope. Many of us, when we are worried or concerned over some problem or difficult situation, cannot see much beyond that concern. But John rises above those limits. There is no doubt that he is concerned over the situation of the churches in the province of Asia. But he faces that concern armed with a vision that includes, not only those seven churches, but also the "twenty-four elders," that is to say, the entire history of Israel and the whole church. Within that history, the tribulations and difficulties of the seven churches, although important, are but an episode. This does not detract from the importance of those tribulations and difficulties, but it does place them in their proper framework. The God who promises salvation and victory to the churches of Asia is the same God the twenty-four elders adore, because it is this God who led Israel out of Egypt and delivered Elisha from the armies of Syria. For that God, the current situation of the churches of Asia is not new or unique. And if the churches of Asia remember that their God is the God of those "twenty-four elders, " they will learn to trust God, as Israel trusted God when crossing the sea, or Daniel in the den of lions.

Do you think that Christians today, as we face problems and difficulties, sufficiently remember that our God has seen God's people through worse times and situations? Do we remember that God is not only our God, but also the God of the twenty-four elders and of all their history?

Act: Go back to the list you made yesterday, of things that cause you fear or concern. On each one of those things, try to remember some moment in the history of the people represented by those "twenty-four elders" (that is to say, the history of Israel and of the Church) when God responded to similar difficulties or concerns. For instance, if what worries you is death, remember Jesus' resurrection. If what worries you is hunger, remember the widow of Zarephath (1 Kings 17:8-16). If what worries you is political or economic oppression, remember the liberation of Israel from the yoke of Egypt. After remembering each of those things, pray: "Thank you, my God, that you are also the God of the ages and that through those ages you have sustained and liberated your people. Thank you that you are always the same, ready to liberate and sustain me."

Third Day: Read Revelation 4:6-11

See: The four "living creatures" remind us of the vision of Ezekiel 1, where there is also something like four living creatures. In Ezekiel's vision, each one of the four living creatures had four faces: the face of a human, the face of a lion, the face of an ox, and the face of an eagle. In John's vision, one of the creatures has a human face, another the face of a lion, and so on. In both visions, the living creatures have many eyes, meaning that they see all things; and they have wings, meaning that they are fast and can be anywhere. Their four faces indicate that they include the whole living creation: humans, wild beasts, domestic animals, and birds. Or, according to other interpreters, the faces indicate that they have all virtues: human wisdom, the strength of an ox, the valor of a lion, and the ability to soar like an eagle.

In any event, the important point is that the four living crea-tures, like the twenty-four elders, even while being so powerful, serve and adore the one who is on the throne, God. What we have here is an image of the heavenly worship that proclaims that the people of God (Israel and the church) and the entire liv-ing creation adore the one who sits on the throne.

Judge: When in the midst of our problems we find ourselves not trusting in God, quite often that is because we have too small a notion of God. Yesterday we saw that God is not only our God, but also the God of the "twenty-four elders" and of the whole history that they represent. Today we see that God is also God of creation, including the beasts and the birds of the sky. The living creatures that represent the whole creation worship God, just as the twenty-four elders adore God. Once again, could it be that our God is too small, and that for that reason we do not trust God with our problems and difficulties?

Act: Pray: My God, as I move ahead in this study of Revelation, I confess that many times I forget your power that encompasses all, your love that promises all, your fidelity that fulfills all. Help me, as you helped John, to have a glimpse of your greatness, so that I may trust you more fully and serve you more faithfully. Through Jesus Christ, my Savior. Amen.

Fourth Day: Read Revelation 5:1-4

See: In John's vision, there is a book in God's right hand. The right hand is the hand of execution and of performance. The book is the plan of God for the ages, what God will do throughout time. But for the time being the book is sealed. This means that nobody can read it. It also means that the plan itself cannot unfold, for it is only as the scroll unrolls that the plan of God will be unwrapped.

The angel's cry indicates that someone of exceptional power is necessary to open the book, and that such a one does not appear. John weeps, not because his curiosity has been frustrated, but because as long as the book remains shut the plan of God's will not move toward its final fulfillment. What is necessary is somebody who is able to set in motion the plan of the ages—or, what is the same, someone worthy of breaking the seven seals that keep it closed.

Judge: John's weeping when he sees that nobody can open the book is akin to humankind's pain as long as the book remains closed, as long as there is no hope of redemption, as long as somebody is not able to unleash the plan of the ages. John weeps because as a Christian he knows that the plan of God is a plan of love, and now it appears that such a plan will be frustrated.

Is the plan of God so important for us that when something seems to frustrate it we weep? John weeps because he hopes the plan of God will include the redemption of the suffering churches of Asia. Do we weep upon seeing that there are so many people, so many institutions that reject or simply ignore God's plan of peace and love? Do we hurt when we see that God's love seems to be absent from someone's life?

Act: Look around you. You know that the plan of God is a plan of love and redemption. However, there are around us many places and people where that plan seems to be frustrated. There are millions who do not believe. There are millions who abuse other millions. There are churches that seem to be about to disappear. There are problems in the church. Weep and lament over the world, over the church, over yourself. There are so many dark corners where the love of God is not followed and obeyed! Write down your lament in the form of a prayer that God will intervene so that there is justice and peace and love.

Fifth Day: Read Revelation 5:5-6

See: There is only One who can open the roll—and he can do it because of his victory. Although John does not tell us yet, it is clear that this victory is the one that Jesus has achieved through his resurrection, by conquering the power of the death. For the time being, what we are told is that the victory has been achieved by "the Lion of the tribe of Judah, the root of David"— that is to say, David's descendant.

But when John looks for that lion, what he sees is a lamb! Even more, what he sees is a lamb "standing as if it had been slaughtered." This is a clear reference to the crucifixion and resurrection of Jesus. The Lamb has seven horns and seven eyes. Since the number seven is a sign of perfection, and the horns a sign of power, what we are being told is that the Lamb that was slaughtered, but still lives, has the fullness of power. The seven eyes of the Lamb are the "seven spirits of God"—that is to say, the fullness of the Spirit—that have been "sent out into all the earth." Thus, the Lamb has the fullness of wisdom because he has the fullness of the Spirit of God who visits and knows all things.

Judge: We have read or heard this passage so often that we do not realize the dramatic contrast between two of the titles that are given to Jesus: he is the Lion of the tribe of Judah, as well as the Lamb that was slain. When we think of a lion, what comes to mind is a powerful and terrible wild animal that imposes its authority through fear. When we think of a lamb, what comes to mind is just the opposite. The lamb is a quiet and inoffensive animal that can barely defend itself. The contrast between these two images indicates that Jesus has won a great victory, such a great victory that by virtue of it he has the power to open the book sealed with seven seals. But he has won that victory, not like a lion that rushes upon the enemy to destroy it, but rather as a lamb that offers its life.

This does not mean that Jesus is not powerful. The vision says it clearly: the lamb has seven horns—the fullness of power. But such power has been gained by means of self-surrender and even death. This victory, in contrasting to the victories of armies and of lions, is a victory of love, of giving of self, of suffering. Undoubtedly, this image is presented to Christians in the suffering churches of Asia so that they may know that quite possibly through those very sufferings that seem to be a sign of defeat they are achieving the greatest of victories. Like the Lamb, Christians must conquer by means of love and giving of self.

Is this how you and your church face whatever difficulties or enemies you or the church may have?

Act: Review in your mind your actions and reactions during this past week. When somebody opposed you, did you respond in love? Or on the contrary, did you respond to criticism or contempt or hatred with the same coin?

Write down some recent episode in your life when you had to face somebody. Ask yourself: What could I have done so that the sign of the Lamb would have been seen in my actions and attitudes? Resolve that from now on, when criticism or opposition arouses anger in you, you will stop to think about what attitude will be a more truthful reflection of the love of the Lamb. (But at the same time, remember that the Lamb is powerful. It is not a matter of compromising your faith or of letting injustice continue by not opposing it. It is rather a matter of facing injustice with a greater justice than is current.)

Sixth Day: Read Revelation 5:7-8

See: The Lamb takes the book from the right hand of God. He takes it directly from the hand of God, without intermediary. This indicates that the Lamb has a dignity equal to God's. In the whole book of Revelation nobody else, only the Lamb, approaches the throne to the point of being able to touch God.

This divine authority of the Lamb is acknowledged in verse 8, where the twenty-four elders and the four living creatures prostrate themselves in worship before the Lamb. (Tomorrow we will look at the hymn they sing to him.) God alone is worthy of adoration. Thus, the Lamb has divine authority—it is God.

The twenty-four elders and the four living creatures adore the Lamb with harps. But they also have in their hands "golden bowls full of incense, which are the prayers of the saints." Here we see another case of what was said before, when comparing Revelation with a drama that takes place on two levels. These two levels are interconnected. The prayers that the saints—that is to say, the believers—rise to the celestial throne and join with the praise that God receives from the Lamb, the twenty-four elders (both the old Israel and the new one that the church is), and from the four living creatures–all that lives.

Judge: We sometimes imagine that the worship we offer to God is no more than our own act of praise. Quite often, as I worship, I think that God is right there with me and that therefore my praise goes directly to God. It is good and proper to think this. But it is also important that we think of our praise rising to heaven and joining a choir of praise such as we cannot even imagine. Praise and prayer are powerful because God is among us. And they are also powerful because they ascend to heaven and join the choir of the ages.

Act: Pray that, when you worship, you may have at least a glimpse of how worship rises to heaven. Pray with the consciousness that your prayer, though silent, joins the prayers of your congregation and they together join the heavenly choir as it sings the song of all the ages.

Seventh Day: Read Revelation 5:9-14

See: We come now to the song of praise that the entire creation intones in honor of the Lamb. The hymn begins declaring the authority of the Lamb to open the seals—an authority that the Lamb has achieved by virtue of its expiatory sacrifice. It is a beautiful hymn of praise that has inspired many Christian hymns. But perhaps the most interesting point in this hymn is the way it describes the scope of the power of the Lamb.

In the first place, the hymn stresses the universal character of the people that the Lamb has redeemed, the church. They come "from every tribe and language and people and nation." Six other times we will find in Revelation a similar phrase, and its intent is always to underscore the scope of the events that are described. Here it is the redemptive work of the Lamb, and therefore what the hymn stresses is that this redemptive work crosses all the barriers of tribe, language, and so forth. For the faithful of the churches in Asia, this would be important, because the Roman Empire was proud of having united many tribes and nations; but now they are told that the Lamb has redeemed people of every tribe and language and people and nation—that is to say that the scope of its redemptive work is even more extensive than the reach of the Roman Empire. And, to emphasize the authority and freedom that this gives to believers, the hymn continues, saying that the Lamb has made them "a kingdom of priests," and that they will reign on earth. Remember that the vast majority of believers in the churches of Asia were slaves, poor craftsmen, women who had to work with their hands to make a living. The fury of the vast and powerful Roman Empire had been unleashed—or was about to be unleashed—against them. Who were they that they could hope to resist such fury? The answer of Revelation is clear: the faithful ones have been made rulers and priests, and they will reign next to God and to the Lamb.

Second, verse 11 tells us that among those who sang this hymn were "myriads of myriads" of angels. This is something that we may find difficult to understand, but according to this hymn the angels also sing praises to the Lamb that was slaughtered, as if they too had stood in need of redemption. At any rate, they join their praise with that of the saints from all tribes and nations.

Third, those who join in this hymn are not only human beings and angels, but the whole of creation: "every creature in heaven and on earth and under the earth and in the sea." We sometimes think that it is only rational creatures who praise God. But here we see that the praise of God is a universal song that includes not only humans and angels, but also all that has been created. (Remember the end of the hymn in Philippians 2:10: "every knee should bend, in heaven and on earth and under the earth.")

Finally, Jesus' authority includes all forms of authority (notice that once again a list of seven is given): "he is worthy ... to receive power and wealth and wisdom and might and honor and glory and blessing!"

In short, there is nothing that the redemptive work of Jesus does not touch. Maybe some rebel against him. Certainly, as we shall see later on, many will rebel, and at the end will be destroyed. But even those who rebel do so against the one who is properly their Lord and Redeemer, the slaughtered Lamb.

Judge: We have come back to the theme of the universal dominion of Jesus, the Christ. Do you truly believe that Jesus is Lord of all the things, even of those that rebel against him? Or do you think that there are some things that have nothing to do with Jesus and with his redemptive work as the slaughtered Lamb? Do you believe that the Christian faith has to do only with religious matters and with eternal life? If so, your faith is very different from the one that is proclaimed here by the elders, by the four living creatures, by the angels, and by the entire creation. What Revelation says is that the cross and resurrection of Jesus Christ—the immolation of the Lamb—is of such importance that every other event and every other fact must be seen and measured with reference to it.

Do you believe that such a message would be a word of comfort for the churches of Asia that lived under the threat of persecution and under all sorts of pressure? Do you believe that such a message is of comfort and strength for today's churches, many of which have withdrawn to the safe environment of the purely religious, while the world seems to continue drifting into destruction? Do you believe that if we took the universal scope of the power of Jesus Christ more seriously our attitudes would be different?

Act: Make a list of areas of your life where it is difficult for you to see the presence of Jesus Christ (for instance, politics, trade, television programs, and so on). Now consider how Christ may be present there, and what may be your responsibility as a follower of the Lamb who was slain, to make his presence more evident. Discuss this with other people. Write down your reflections.

For Group Study

After discussing what is said above, ask the group to make a list of things that, according to this text, praise the Lamb. (They can be such things as mountains, rivers, birds, fish, Christians who died in the faith, and so forth). Assign to each participant one of these roles (one could be the mountains, another the rivers, and so on). Ask each person to imagine how a hymn of praise would sound coming from each of the things named (for instance, the voice of the mountain would be strong and deep, that of the rivers soft and sibilant, and so on). Finally, give each one the opportunity to repeat the hymn that we are studying (Revelation 5:12 and 13*b*) with the voice he or she has have been assigned (the mountain with a mountain voice, the bird with a bird voice, and so forth). Or after having each one think of the voice appropriate use to personify what has been assigned, have the whole group read together, but with their different assigned voices, the hymn that all creation sings.

W E E K
FOUR

First Day: Read Revelation 6:1-4

See: We come now to the moment when the Lamb begins to open the seven seals. In the course of the week we will see that, while the first seals are described very briefly, the others take up much more space, to the point that the seventh seal is not broken until much later.

In a way, the first two seals tell the political history of what was then the Roman province of Asia. Until shortly before the advent of Christianity, the region had suffered repeated invasions by the Persians. But then the might of Rome prevailed, and now the whole area was part of the Roman Empire. The first horseman is mounted on a white horse, symbol of victory, and armed with a bow. Such was the traditional armament of the Persians, and therefore the first readers of Revelation would understand quite readily that this was a reference to the Persian invaders of the past, who were still a very real threat. The second horseman rides a red horse, the color of blood and of violence, and in his hand is the sort of great sword that, as we have already seen, was a symbol of Roman authority.

Judge: The churches of Asia were in a difficult political situation. All were under the rule of Rome, which claimed to have brought peace to the region. One in the ways in which Rome stayed in power in that area was by reminding its inhabitants of the cruelties that the Persians had perpetrated in the past, and the danger of a new Persian invasion. Often those who criticized Roman government were accused of being sympathetic toward the Persians.

John's vision, however, implies that both empires produce

death and destruction. One takes a crown, as a sign that its poli-cy policy is one one of open conquest. The other has the power of removing or destroying peace, which is in open contradiction to the Roman claim of having brought peace to the region. In a situation in which the rulers as well as much of society insisted that those who did not accept all the commands and the values of Rome might well have Persian sympathies, John's vision exposes the destructive power of both.

Can you think of any parallel cases today? Until a few years ago, while the Cold War was at its height, many who for what-ever reason dared criticize some of the actions of the Western powers were immediately accused of communist leanings. Today that particular situation no longer exists. But there are still those who demand absolute loyalty to their country and its policies, claiming that otherwise one supports some enemy, either real or supposed. This happens both at the international level and at the local level. If somebody criticizes the policies of the United States in the Middle East, they are considered soft on terrorism. Likewise, if somebody protests against a local indus-try that pollutes the environment, many consider that person subversive. Does this help you understand why early Christians were considered subversive and were persecuted?

Act: List some of the authorities in your context that are tempted to demand unconditional loyalty. These may include a national government, a political party, the company for which you work, or even the church or its leaders. Think of the good that each one of these do, and resolve to support them. But think also of their mistakes and resolve to point them out. Pray, asking for the wisdom to discern between one and the other, and for the power to be faithful and obedient.

Second Day: Read Revelation 6:5-8

See: We come now to the third and fourth seals. The third seal is opened to reveal a mounted horseman on a black horse—a sym-bol of death—with a scale in his hand—a symbol of trade. A voice is heard complaining about the price of wheat and barley, while wine and oil are specially protected.

This vision refers to the impact of trade on agriculture and on the lives of the poor of the area. The ownership of land was increasingly concentrated in the hands of large landowners who rarely lived on the land. For such landowners, the most productive use of land was to plant olive trees and vineyards, for oil and wine could be sold at a high price in Rome and other large cities. The result was that grain became scare, and the price of bread became prohibitive. The voice complains that a day's wage does not suffice to buy two pounds of wheat. Since this is unhulled wheat, it hardly suffices for a loaf of bread. How will a worker be able to feed his family—to say nothing of providing shelter and clothing, paying taxes, and such? Emperor Domitian had become aware of this problem and had issued a decree limiting the use of land for vines and olive trees. But the protest of the landowners was such that the edict had to be revoked. In short, it was the poor who suffered as a result of the policies and the enrichment of the powerful.

It is to this that the voice refers that is heard as the third horseman emerges: "A quart of wheat for day's pay, and three quarts of barley for a day's pay, but do not damage the olive oil and the wine!"

The fourth horse is yellow or pale. This is the color of mystery. Death cannot always be explained by political events (as could the first two horsemen) or economic policies (as the third). There is also this fourth horseman, mysterious and powerful, that also has great power to harm.

Judge: The book of Revelation does not simplify problems. If the first two horsemen speak of political realities, the third deals with economic issues. And the fourth reminds us that, even apart from bad policies and bad economic practices, death and destruction still remain. It is not a matter of imagining that everything can be explained simplistically on the basis of political circumstances or economic analysis.

Yet, Revelation does reflect an economic analysis of the situation of its readers. If you made a similar analysis, what conclusions would you reach? Consider, for instance: What are the most serious problems in your community (for instance, drugs, lack of housing, deficiencies in education, insufficient support for the elderly)? Who or what benefits from that situation? (Or, in other words, if the church began a campaign to eradicate that problem, who would oppose it most vigorously? What powers are the counterpart of the black horse in your community?)

Act: Discuss your conclusions with other people in your church. Together, try to determine what actions to take to eradicate those problems of your community. Do this with full awareness that such actions will be opposed by today's counterpart of the horseman on the black horse.

Third Day: Read Revelation 6:9-11

See: When each of the first four seals is opened, one of the famous four horsemen of the Apocalypse comes forth. What happens at the opening of the fifth seal is very different. John sees under the altar the souls of all the martyrs—"those who had been slaughtered for the word of God and for the testimony they had given." Since John sees a continuity between the message of God to Israel and the fulfillment of that message in the proclamation of the church, one may suppose that these martyrs include both those Jews who in the past have suffered for their faith and Christians who have suffered more recently. All those souls cry out to God, calling for the day of the final victory, when they will receive justice and those who persecuted and oppressed them will be destroyed. The answer is surprising: the end has to wait until the sufferings of new generations are completed. There are other people who must join this number of martyrs, and it is necessary to wait for them.

Judge: Remember that this book was originally written as a message from the Lord to the churches of Asia Minor, threatened with persecution and death. What is more, some people had already died for their faith. Therefore, the question of the souls of the martyrs under the altar is the same question that would be asked by the faithful in places such as Smyrna, Pergamum, and Philadelphia. And the answer is not a date. On the contrary, the answer is simply that there must still be more suffering for those who are on earth. All that the believers in Smyrna, Pergamum, Philadelphia, and the other churches are being told is that the Lord is aware of their sufferings and that in the end they will be vindicated. What such believers must do is to continue being faithful, although for the time being it seems that those who oppose them are more powerful than the church and its members. The final word will be the Lord's.

Act: Most of us today do not suffer persecution and opposition like that confronting those churches of Asia Minor. But we de suffer the constant temptation to think that the present powers are more powerful than God. Go back to what you wrote in your notebook the first day of last week. Have you acted since then on the conviction that indeed God is more powerful than all those things? Write down what you believe you must do so that your actions will be more in line with that vision of the great power of God. Pray for the power to be faithful.

Fourth Day: Read Revelation 6:12-17

See: The first five seals took little space—each one a matter of a few verses. But the sixth will take the rest of chapter 6 and all of 7. It is with the opening of this seal that the horror scenes begin to unfold that have become so famous in the book of Revelation. The metaphors are overwhelming: the sun becomes black like the sackcloth that was made from certain wools of the region; the moon becomes like blood; the stars fall like fruit from a shaken fig tree; the sky disappears like a scroll being rolled up; and the mountains and the islands are removed.

Facing such catastrophes, people seek to escape by hiding in caves. Notice that the vision underlines the panic of the powerful: "the kings of the earth and the magnates and the generals and the rich and the powerful, and everyone, slave and free." Nobody escapes the great catastrophe.

The fact that all these people hide in caves and among the rocks of the mountains suggests that John is speaking in metaphoric language, because we have just been told that the mountains had been removed. In any event, all these people prefer death rather than having to face the wrath of the Lamb.

What all this indicates is that the time of vindication that the souls of the martyrs cried for has finally arrived when the fifth seal is opened. This is why the text underscores the panic of the powerful, who are in fact those who have persecuted and oppressed the faithful. But those who are not powerful are not exempt: "everyone, slave and free."

Judge: This book was written as a word of comfort and affirmation for Christians in the province of Asia who suffered persecution and all kinds of economic and social pressure. In contrast, when we read it today, many see it as a book of fright. The truth is that, apart from the Psalms, this is the book of the Bible that has inspired most hymns. And in spite of that, when today we say that something is "apocalyptic," we mean that it is tragic and catastrophic.

Why is it that a book that for its first readers was a word of comfort causes terror in us? Could it be that our place in the world and in society is very different from the position of those early Christians? Those churches in Asia looked upon the cataclysms announced in Revelation as a metaphor for their final vindication. It is difficult for us today to see things in the same light. Could it be that we have such an investment in the present order that we do not want it to pass away? Could it be that our perspective comes closer to that of "the kings of the earth and the magnates and the generals and the rich and the powerful"?

If we really saw and experienced the wickedness of the present order and were among the many who suffer as a consequence of that order would we not see its end with the same joy with which the first readers of Revelation were invited to see it?

Act: Review verse 15, making a list of those things described as *powerful*: kings, magnates, the rich, generals. In each one of these cases, are there others who suffer because of the power of such people? Think, for example, of the equivalent of today's kings: the dictators, and all the people who suffer under their boot. Think of the magnates of today, and whose lives they rule or affect; think of who are rich and who are poor. In each of those situations, to what group do you belong? What group does your church represent? Whose interests do you and your church serve? Propose to always take the side of those who suffer, not of those who cause suffering; only thus will you be able to stand in the day of the wrath of the Lamb.

Fifth Day: Read Revelation 7:1-3

See: The series of metaphors of destruction and vengeance continues. It is important that we understand that what is described here is not a detailed and orderly program for how and when the end of the world will come. If we try to read Revelation in that way, as many do today, and if we do it carefully and sincerely, soon we will encounter problems. For instance, after all the catastrophes that are described in the passage that we studied yesterday, the angels are ordered not to harm the earth. Here, as well as later on in the book, it appears that the sea, the earth, and the trees are as they were before, and as if there were still a sun, a moon, a sky, and stars, even though we were told earlier that all this was destroyed, or at least drastically transformed. Once again, we should not read Revelation the way one reads a television program, to know exactly what comes next. That is not the purpose of the book. Its purpose is rather to let us know that the Lord is God above all the false gods, and that God knows and will vindicate all the sufferings and difficulties that Christians must face if they are to be faithful.

In any event, what is described here is an absolute calm in the winds. The four angels stop the four winds. It is a stillness that produces anxiety and expectation, the absolute calm that seems to announce the coming storm.

But the storm is held back because it is necessary to mark those who have been servants of God. They will be marked with the seal of God that the angel that rises from the east holds in its hand. Remember that at that time it was customary to mark the forehead of some slaves to indicate to whom they belonged. (Later on we will see that other people are marked with the seal of the beast.) Notice also that this passage is parallel to what we are told in Exodus 12, about how the Lord slew all the firstborn of Egypt but the angel of destruction did not touch those who had marked their houses with the blood of the lamb.

Judge: The angel must seal the servants of God. What this means is that it will place on them a sign that they belong to God. In Revelation, this is what salvation means: to belong to God, to be sealed or marked with the name of God.

It is important that we see this dimension of salvation, because too often we are promised a "cheap" salvation that does not require of us more than that we "accept" what God offers us. It is true that all that is required is to accept what God offers us; but what God offers us is to be our owner, to seal us with God's name, to use us as it suits God.

Do you belong to God, and do you act as one who belongs to God? Or are you rather your own owner, doing what you find most pleasurable or convenient, and serving God only when it suits you? Does your church belong to God? Or are there some members who believe that because they give more or because they attend more frequently or because they have been members for a long time, the church belongs to them? What would it mean, to be a church sealed with the name of God?

Act: Make a list of what you are and what you have (for instance, "teacher," "father," "money," "time," "education"). Consider how you can put each of the roles listed in the service of God, because if you belong to God, all that you are and all you have belongs to God. Write down your reflections. In a few days, read again what you wrote, to see if such reflections have truly changed your life.

Sixth Day: Read Revelation 7:4-8

See: This passage has been much discussed, as if it meant that there are only 144,000 who will be saved. But it is necessary to notice two things in this respect: the first one is that the passage refers to those sealed "out of every tribe of the people of Israel." In other words, the text is only speaking of the descendants of Israel. (Remember what we have said previously, that in Revelation the people of God is both Israel and the church, and both are represented by the twenty-four elders.) The second thing that it is necessary to note is that the number 144,000 is a way of saying that a great multitude—the fullness of the descendants of Israel who have been faithful—is counted among those sealed. Indeed, twelve is a number that indicates perfection, wholeness. Twelve times twelve is 144. Thus, the figure 144,000, like so many other things in Revelation, must not be taken literally. It indicates rather that the fullness of salvation has come to Israel.

Judge: Place yourself in the situation of the first addressees of this book. As we have seen when studying the seven letters to the seven churches, for those churches the question of their relationship to Judaism was a serious problem. On the one hand, there were Jews who said that those who believed in Jesus Christ were false Jews. On the other hand, there were Gentiles converted to Christianity who insisted that to be a Christian it was necessary to obey all the laws of Israel. It would be exasperating for those churches and their members to find themselves attacked from both sides. Now John tells them that salvation is also for that enormous number from among the tribes of Israel. What is more, it is the angel of God who seals these people. Their salvation is not something that depends on the churches. The saving work of the Lamb goes beyond what its followers may imagine. These descendants of Israel will be sealed with the seal of God, and they will be saved by the blood of the Lamb. How this can be, we are not told. And we are not told precisely so that we may know that the work and the mercy of God are higher and more mysterious than anything we may imagine or explain.

Act: Pray: Lord, I do not understand the mysteries of your wisdom, or the mystery of your purposes. I ask that you be my teacher, not so that you may clear up every mystery, but so I may learn to trust in you. Seal me with your seal, so that I may be perfectly yours. Everything else I leave in your hands, knowing that you will act according to your great and wondrous mercy. Amen.

Seventh Day: Read Revelation 7:9-17

See: Now John sees another multitude. It does not come from among the descendants of Israel, but "from every nation, from all tribes and peoples and languages." In other words, these people now include all sorts of Gentiles. Their white clothes and their palms are a sign of victory. (At a later time, a palm branch would come to be the sign of the martyrs, those who had attained the greatest victory possible.) All these people praise God and the Lamb to whom salvation belongs. And they are joined by the multitude of angels, the twenty-four elders, and the four living creatures, who say "Amen" to what the choir of the redeemed sings, and they too worship God.

Then one of the elders explains to John that these people with white clothes and palms of victory are "they who have come out of the great ordeal; they have washed their robes and made them white in the blood of the Lamb." In other words, they are those who have remained faithful through difficulties and persecution. (Notice the interesting metaphor, according to which the blood of the Lamb whitens the clothes of its followers.) For that reason not only are they in the presence of God, but also God shelters them—that is to say, covers them with divine protection. The result of that protection is that they are not hungry or thirsty, and that they are not burned by the sun or scorched by any heat, "for the Lamb at the center of the throne will be their shepherd." Once again, the metaphor is surprising: the Lamb becomes a shepherd! (Remember that other surprising passage, where it turns out that the Lion of Judah is a lamb.) These words remind us of Psalm 23, where this shepherd/lamb leads us beside still waters. In Revelation, as a final sign of divine favor and care, the faithful are promised that "God will wipe away every tear from their eyes." Here the imagery becomes tender, reminding us of a mother who wipes the tears of a hurting child. All this has been promised to those who have washed their robes in the blood of the Lamb, and who have been faithful.

Judge: Naturally, the purpose of this scene is to invite readers of Revelation to see themselves as part of that multitude from every people, nation, and language that worships the Lord and whom the Lamb shepherds. Amid their tribulations, Christians in Pergamum, Sardis, Thyatira, and the other churches would know that the Lord of Lords who sits on the throne, and the Lamb who stands by the throne, were watching over them, and in the end God's sheltering love would cover them. With that promise, they would have the strength necessary to remain firm amid persecution or any other difficulty they might have to face.

Some have said that the hope of eternal life leads people to be passive in their acceptance of the present situation. It is true that sometimes the powerful have used that hope to tell those whom they oppress that they do not have to oppose oppression or to protest, because in the end they will go to heaven. But the opposite is also true: the hope of life eternal may give those who have such hope an irresistible power and fortitude. When early Christians became convinced that, even if the Roman authorities took their lives, in the end they would reign with God, and that there was nothing that those apparently powerful authorities could do to impede it, they became an irresistible force. Many men and women were killed because they refused to give up their faith. Many others were tortured, exiled, or condemned to forced labor in the mines. But even so, they remained firm. The Roman Empire roared, threatened, and destroyed; but in the end it had to give in. Such is the power of faith!

Could it be that when we today agree too readily to the demands of society this is in fact a sign that we lack faith—that John's vision has lost its clarity and certainty? Could it be that in fact we are not so sure that the Lamb will shepherd us and that God will wipe away all tears from our eyes?

When the church conforms itself too much to the patterns of society—when, for instance, it seems to think that by just having more money it will have more success, or when it does not dare protest against injustices—could it be that it has lost John's vision?

If we seriously believe that God will wipe away all our tears, and that the Lamb will shepherd us and take us to fresh waters, will we not be more daring as we face those who seem to control humankind's destiny in the present age?

Act: Go back to what you wrote three days ago (the fourth day of this week) about how you could opt for the weak and the oppressed rather than the strong and the oppressors. What have you done in this regard? Pray, asking God to make you more faithful, to give you the power to speak the truth and to do what is right in every circumstance, even though the price may be high. Ask for the faith and trust in God to take such risks, because without them there is no Christian obedience.

For Group Study

Review with the group all that has been studied since the sixth seal was opened (starting from 6:12). In that review, ask the group to make a list of those Revelation says should fear the wrath of the Lamb, and another list of what is said about those who have no reason to fear it.

After making those two lists, invite the group to discuss what elements in each of them describe us. Are we among those who should fear the wrath of the Lamb, or among those who will be shepherded by him? What must we do to make sure that we are among this second group and not among the first one?

W E E K

FIVE

First Day: Read Revelation 8:1

See: Imagine the situation. All the members of the church of Smyrna are gathered, while one of them reads aloud the book that John has sent them. Up to now, after the seven letters to the seven churches, the whole book has focused on the seven seals that close the great scroll and that the Lamb opens one by one. The audience has been eagerly awaiting the opening of the seventh seal. If the sixth spoke of earthquakes, of the sky rolled up as a parchment, of stars falling like fruit off a shaken tree, what would the seventh bring?

The reader finally comes to the seventh seal. The whole congregation listens attentively. Will there be fire and destruction? Will there be an unequaled hymn of praise? Certainly the end draws near!

But the reader says: "When the Lamb opened the seventh seal, there was silence in heaven for about half an hour." At that point, a great sigh must have been heard among the congregation. We were wrong. We have not come to the end yet. Our God is sovereign and free, and therefore God's times are unpredictable. Instead of trying to guess what will come later, what those believers in Smyrna must do is to be faithful and to let God surprise them in unpredictable and mysterious, yet loving, ways.

Judge: Through the centuries, there have been people who have tried to read Revelation as if it were a program in which what will happen next is announced. Perhaps as the churches in Asia first heard the reading of this sublime book, some imagined that they already knew what would come next. If so, God repeatedly surprised them! In the ancient church, as persecution grew worse, there were those who tried to figure out dates and events on the basis of Revelation and therefore decided that the Lord would come in the next twenty years. But they were wrong. Then, when Emperor Constantine became a Christian, there were those who said that surely now the end was about to come, and tried to prove it with quotes from Revelation. But they too were wrong. When the Germanic "barbarians" invaded the Roman Empire, there were those who saw in those events the fulfillment of the prophecies of Revelation and declared that the Lord would come in the year 500. But they too were wrong. When the year one thousand approached, there were those who saw in the events of the time sure signs that this would be the date of the return of the Lord. But they too were wrong. Later, other people have pointed out other dates: 1260, 1580, 1945, 1975, 2000. But they have all been wrong.

Late in the nineteenth century, C. S. Scofield proposed an interpretation of Revelation that sought to show how each one of its prophecies was being fulfilled. But he too was wrong.

All these people were wrong, not because they made errors in their calculations, but because they imagined that Revelation was an outline of future events—a sort of program for the last times that believers could follow much as one follows the program for a concert or the TV Guide. But Revelation is not that. Revelation is the Word of God. It is the Word of God for all times. It was the Word of God for those who first heard its reading in the churches of Asia. It was the Word of God for believers who were being persecuted in the third century. It was the Word of God for the reformers in the sixteenth century. And it is the Word of God for us. But it is the Word of God not because it helps us figure out God's mysterious plans and times, as if God had presented us with a puzzle, but because it calls us to be faithful in all circumstances and in every difficulty.

If those who heard the reading of the letter for the first time were surprised when hearing that after the seventh seal what comes is a period of silence, what this teaches us is that this book has been given to us not so that we may guess or try to discover what comes next, but so that we may see, based on the eternal purposes of God, what must be the nature of our obedience here and now.

Act: Pray: Do not permit, Lord that I may read your sacred Word merely out of curiosity, as if trying to discover some hidden secret. Help me remember at every step that your Word is a call to obedience, and not a puzzle to decipher; that it is not up to me to know the times and the seasons that are solely in your will (Acts 1:7); that it is up to me to be obedient, and to be a witness to your love and your mercy until the end of the world—no matter when this may be. Until then, keep me under your wings of mercy. Amen.

Second Day: Read Revelation 8:2-5

See: If readers of Revelation imagine that what John is saying is that the end is near, and that it is only necessary to wait a few more days, the structure of the book itself soon will force them to think otherwise. We were reading about the seven seals, and one might have thought that with the opening of the seventh seal the end would come. But no: now that the seventh seal is finally open what appears is a series of seven angels, each one with a trumpet, and we must now wait for the blasts of the seven trumpets. And if we imagine that at the seventh trumpet the end will come, we err again, for after the seven trumpets there are seven cups of wrath. If we remember that the number seven is a symbol of fullness, what we have here is $7 \times 7 \times 7$—that is to say, a triple fullness! The end comes closer, yes, but not in such a way that we can say that it is around the next corner.

The verses we are studying serve as an introduction to the seven trumpets. In the Jewish tradition people spoke of the "seven angels" of the presence, the main angels or archangels that surround the throne of God. Combining what was said in several different books, these seven angels were given the names of Michael, Gabriel, Raphael, Uriel, Raguel, Sariel, and Remiel.

Of the seven, Michael is the only one mentioned by name in Revelation (12:7). In the Bible, trumpets are a sign of divine intervention or an announcement of God's action. Thus, what will follow each of the seven trumpets is an announcement or warning to those who do not believe. They will be terrible warnings, but their purpose is not so much destruction as capturing the attention of those tempted to unfaithfulness.

What is said about the golden censer and the prayers of the saints reminds us that the worship of believers on earth joins the worship that takes place in heaven, and that it all rises to the throne of God. What is more, the prayers of the saints return to earth, although now in the form of thunder and rumblings and flashes of lightning and earthquakes.

Judge: The purpose of all this is not to explain natural disasters. John is not asking, for instance, Why are there earthquakes? What interests John and his readers is how believers are to respond to all the pressures and oppressions to which they are subjected. How are they to understand their own worship and praise? What are they to think about those who now oppress them and make them suffer injustice? Will such people go unpunished? Certainly not. Their punishment will be such that thunder and earthquake are but warnings of the anger to come.

This may seem an exaggeration to many of us, an unworthy spirit of vengeance on the part of those who call themselves by the name of Christ. But the fact is that, if we look around, we will soon see that life without faith always ends up in tragedy. Either through disasters such as earthquakes, plagues, or floods, or merely by the passing of time, all oppressors will end up dead. Thus, those who live only to exploit and to oppress others actually do not live for anything. And the same is true of those who live only to live. That supposed life is but death; and when physical death finally comes, such lives turn out to be nothing but death and vanity.

Thus, like the trumpets that the seven angels blow, each death and each tragedy, each earthquake and each disaster around us, are so many warnings, so many calls to obedience. From a certain point of view, they are one more opportunity than we are given for reflection and repentance.

Act: Give thanks to God for so many warnings and signs that have been given us. Ask for forgiveness for so many times when you have been deaf to such warnings. When reading today's newspaper or listening to the news, try to see in them further warnings and calls from God.

Third Day: Read Revelation 8:6-9

See: As in the case of the first seals, the first trumpets follow one after the other rather quickly. In these four verses we are told what happens when the first two angels blow their trumpets. The first one brings destruction on the earth, so a third of the trees and all the grass are destroyed. The second brings destruction on the sea, so a third of the sea becomes blood, and a third of all ships on the ocean are destroyed, as well as a third of all the living beings that are in the sea.

The reason the destruction is not total is that each one of these trumpets is a warning so that unbelievers may repent. Remember that the horseman that appeared upon the opening of the fourth seal had power over a fourth of the earth. Now, most of the disasters that follow the first trumpets affect a third of the whole. Thus the warnings go *in crescendo*.

The destructive warnings that follow each of the first five trumpets (and in chapter 16 the cups of wrath) remind us the plagues that God employed in order to convince Pharaoh that he must let Israel go. The significance of this parallelism is that Revelation compares the Roman Empire and its political and social order with Egypt—and elsewhere also with Babylon. Just as God liberated Israel from the yoke of Egypt by means of a series of plagues, so will God liberate the church from persecution on the part of the Roman Empire by means of a series of plagues—and these will be even more disastrous than those that scourged Egypt. Just as the plagues announced the end of oppression in Egypt, and led to the death of Pharaoh, so

Revelation announces the liberation from the present condition of oppression, and the fall of Rome.

Judge: It is frequently said that the church should not get into politics. This may well be true, if by politics is meant only the conflicts between parties and candidates. But politics is much more than that. Politics is the way in which a society distributes the resources available among the entire community—money, food, land, education, power, and so on. For instance, according to diverse political positions the natural resources should be used in different ways. Some would argue that whoever owns something may use it as the owner sees fit, even if such use affects or destroys the environment. Others would say that it is more important to protect the environment than to allow the owner of a property to exploit it freely. Something similar happens with regard to education. Some believe that the state should provide quality public education equally to all citizens. Others argue that the state does not have such an obligation, because education is a privilege for which each individual should pay. With regard to immigration, some hold that immigrants are generally undesirable and that therefore a nation should close its borders, while others claim that immigration enriches the country and should not be prohibited All these are questions of justice, and therefore whoever seeks to be a responsible believer must seek to make informed decisions on them, even at the risk of being wrong.

Sometimes there are injustices that come to such a point that a believing person has no option but to oppose them, in the conviction that God also opposes them. Such was the case of the people of Israel in Egypt, or of the churches of Asia to whom John addressed Revelation. John's words about the Roman government and the way in which resources were managed in it would be seen as subversive by any Roman official who read the book and understood it (and it is partly for that reason that the book is written in a mysterious and symbolic language).

Act: Look at your own community to see if there are injustices that the church and its members should oppose because they clearly go against the will of God. It can be the system of rents and administration of apartments, or the educational system, or public transportation, or public health, or others. If you find such an injustice, begin to organize the community of faith to try to make things right.

Fourth Day: Read Revelation 8:10-13

See: The third and fourth trumpets are similar to the two previous ones in that after each one of them the destruction reaches a third of the whole. The third trumpet brings destruction on a third of the waters—which means, of fresh water. It comes in the form of a star that is called "Wormwood." This is a bitter plant that is also poisonous—so poisonous that frequently other nearby plants die. Thus the water is not only bitter but also poisonous.

A detail that is worth mentioning is that a single star falls on a third of the rivers. As a literal description, such a thing is impossible. As poetic metaphor, it presents a powerful image. Once again, Revelation must not be read as prosaic description, but rather as a prophetic and poetic vision.

When the fourth angel blows his trumpet, disaster reaches the sky itself. Remember that the first trumpet brought destruction on the earth, the second on the sea, and the third on the fresh waters. Now the fourth brings catastrophes to the sky: the sun, the moon, and the stars. (Once again, remember that already the sky had rolled up as a parchment, and the sun had become dark. Revelation cannot be read as a program or outline for the final disasters. If we read it as such, it seems to contradict itself repeatedly.)

After the fourth trumpet there is an additional warning, for an angel flies in midheaven announcing three woes on the earth: "Woe, woe, woe to the inhabitants of the earth, at the blasts of the other trumpets that the three angels are about to blow!"

Judge: The warnings are repeated. It would seem that the calamities that follow the first trumpet would be enough so that all would repent. But it is not so. The first trumpet is not enough, nor the second, nor even the third, nor the fourth. Before the blast of the fifth trumpet, God offers an additional warning through this angel that announces destruction. However, as we shall see later on, even then there are still those who reject the plans and the power of God.

What all this shows is that Revelation, far from being, as we often think, a book that presents a vengeful and destructive God, presents a God who wants to forgive and who offers warning after warning. The terror of the woes to come is presented here, not as an indication of the vengeful character of God, but rather as a sign of the hardness of the human heart that refuses to believe in spite of so many and such clear warnings.

Have you not had enough warnings of your own sin and of the necessity of obeying God? Do you believe that, if you were to witness calamities such as those described in Revelation, you would truly turn to God and be more faithful? Sadly, although we tend think so, it is probably not true. Whoever does not believe the daily warnings we all receive will probably not believe even an extraordinary warning.

Act: Pray: Thank you, my God, that in your great mercy you have warned me repeatedly of the end that awaits those who refuse to obey you. Help me respond to those warnings with repentance and faithfulness. I pray in the name Jesus, who has also given us the same warning. Amen.

Fifth Day: Read Revelation 9:1-12

See: As in the case of the seals, the passage on the fifth trumpet is more extensive than the passages on the four previous ones. What happens at the blast of the fourth trumpet reminds us of the eighth plague in Egypt, which was a swarm of locusts (Exodus 10:12-19). But, whereas those were locusts that ate plants, these attack not the vegetation but those who "do not have the seal of God on their foreheads." Also, instead of killing, what they do is to torment these people with a sting like a scorpion's. This will last "five months," which is the length of time that a locust usually lives.

Another passage that serves as background for what is described here is the first two chapters of Joel, where the prophet compares a swarm of locusts to an armed invasion. (If time allows, read those two chapters and you will see the parallels between that passage and this one.) But once again, this swarm of locusts of Revelation is much worse that its antecedents in the Old Testament. These locusts come from the "bottomless pit"— that is to say, the place that will serve as a prison for Satan and his legions. And they are organized with a king to lead them. The author of Proverbs 30:27 marvels that locusts march as an army, even without having a king. But these locusts do have a king, called in Hebrew Abaddon and in Greek Apollyon—both terms meaning destruction. Since Emperor Domitian liked to give himself the name of the god Apollo, it is very probable that there is a reference to him here, and that what was a title of honor for the Emperor, John has turned into a title of horror.

The worst of all is that this terrible plague is but the beginning of the evils that are yet to come, for when the plague passes we are told that "the first woe has passed. There are still two woes to come."

Judge: Notice that once again this is a warning. The locusts hurt and cause pain, but do not kill. And at the end of the fifth trumpet an additional warning appears: there are still two woes to come. Life is full of warnings and episodes that are like the bite of a scorpion, and that should suffice to call us to obedience. We lose something that for us was of great value. A loved one dies. A dream for which we had toiled for years collapses. We face our own death. All this should serve as warning that we have to find the meaning of life somewhere else. And yet, too often we simply go back to the same path as before. The shock of the blow subsides, and our life continues as before. God be thanked that in God's mercy we are given so many warnings, in spite of the hardness of our heart!

Act: Repeat yesterday's prayer. Consider: between yesterday and today, have you remembered the warnings you have received? What aspects of your life are still waiting for you to place them at God's disposal? Write down your reflections. Repeat the same prayer.

Sixth Day: Read Revelation 9:13-19

See: From the point of view of the Roman Empire, and certainly of their authorities in the province of Asia, the most fearsome foreign enemy was Persia. For years and years, war between Rome and Persia had been almost constant, and in spite of the efforts of both contenders the border continued being approximately the course of the river Euphrates. Thus, from the Roman point of view, mentioning the Euphrates immediately brought Persia to mind—much as from the point of view of the United States, mentioning the Río Grande immediately brings Mexico to mind. As a result of their many wars, Roman authorities made every effort to fortify their borders on the Euphrates, or to bolster semi-independent states that served as buffers between the two mighty empires of Persia and Rome.

Thus, John's statement that there are four angels bound at the great river Euphrates means that, although the Romans imagine that their survival is due to their military might, in fact it is God who has not allowed the Persians to sweep into Roman territory. When these four angels are unleashed, an immense army will spill into Roman territory; the number that John gives—two hundred million—is a hyperbole that indicates the enormous size of the invading army.

And, as if their number were not enough, John adds that they had breastplates the color of fire and of sapphire and sulfur and that it was their horses that did the killing, whose mouths spewed fire and sulfur and whose tails had harmful serpent-like heads.

In John's vision, these invaders kill a third of humankind, just as the resulting plagues of the previous trumpets killed or destroyed a third of the trees, a third of the sea, or a third of all the fresh waters.

Judge: Up to this point, in dealing with the repeated warnings that God gives in Revelation, we have tried to apply them to our own life, taking them as warnings addressed to us. But it is also possible to read these warnings from another perspective. If this is the God whom we serve, and this God insists on warning God's enemies over and over again, our task should also be to warn sinners over and over. If God does not give up on these people who have seen so many wonders and suffering, what right have we to claim that we have already given enough warning to our neighbors and friends?

Act: Think of somebody whom you have already given up for lost. Seek that person out and once again speak of the gospel to him or to her. Do it in love. Explain that life without Jesus Christ loses much of its meaning. (Be careful: Too often, when we warn someone else, there is a hidden undercurrent of glee at the evils that may await him or her. That is not a message of love and grace. God's warnings in Revelation are the warnings of a God who wishes for all to be saved. Your warnings and admonitions should also be made in love. Love also requires respect, and therefore you should not try to force the person into agreeing with you.) If that person does not listen, do not give up. Keep on praying for that person. At the next appropriate time, repeat your entreaties and the invitation to believe. Do not become discouraged or give up on that person. God has had so much patience with you! How, then, can you not show a similar patience for others?

Seventh Day: Read Revelation 9:20-21

See: The great calamities that we studied yesterday would remind readers of the last plague of Egypt, when God killed the firstborn of the Egyptians and Pharaoh finally consented to let the people of Israel go. But the contrast is in that, after that plague, Pharaoh consented to the will of God, while after this plague—a worse evil than that of Egypt—people still hold fast to their wickedness and unbelief.

The two verses that we study today list the sorts of wickedness for which these people are not willing to repent. In verse

20, the emphasis is on idolatry, including an entire list of the objects that people worship. In verse 21, the issue is wider in scope, for although one of the practices mentioned could be considered religious (sorceries), the others are common sins of people against each other: murders, fornication, and thefts.

Judge: We have repeatedly seen that the woes that follow the blast of each trumpet come by way of warning so that unbelievers and sinners may repent. But the fact is that they do not repent. Thus, although all these warnings serve to show us the great mercy of God, who does not wish that anybody be lost, the fact is that few are truly converted out of terror.

The church and its members have frequently acted as if the best way to achieve the conversion of those who do not believe was to threaten them with death and hell. Sometimes Christians have tried to take advantage of a tragedy in the life of a person to tell that person that whatever has happened is a punishment from God and that there will be many more such tragedies if the person does not repent. Although it is true that tragedies and disappointments can serve as a warning and call us to repentance, it is also true that, as popular wisdom knows, more flies are caught with honey than with vinegar. Following that metaphor, we should remember that life without God is in itself vinegar, although those who live without God may try to convince themselves that it is honey. Therefore, it is not necessary when announcing the gospel to add more vinegar to those empty and lost lives. What we should do is to show them the honey of the love of God.

Think for a moment of those Christians who first received the book of Revelation. Do you think they became believers out of fear? If something was to be feared in their previous life, it was the power of the authorities and of social pressure. But those people were converted even in spite of that. Why? Probably because the message of the gospel spoke to them of a love that they had not known before. And if at a later point the faith that they had accepted and embraced caused them confrontations with the authorities and even death, they were willing to face everything with the sole purpose of attaining to that Jesus Christ who loved them so.

For those who do not believe, the vacuity of life is warning enough. It is not necessary to threaten them with fire and sulfur, because if that vacuity does not convince them, a thousand earthquakes and floods will not do it either. But, on the other hand, they cannot say later that they did not have enough warning. If not seven trumpets, just about everyone has suffered more than seven shocks that should have served as more than enough warning. Thus, if they do not believe, it is because they refuse to believe and not because God did not give them sufficient warning.

Act: If people around you have already had enough warning of the emptiness of life without God, what you are to do is show them the beauty and the value of life with Jesus Christ. Consider your own behavior toward some of those around you who do not believe. Have you shown them the joy that there is in Jesus Christ? Or have you given them reason to see you as a rigid and bitter person? Returning to the image of honey and vinegar, when those people look at you, will they see honey or will they see vinegar? Write on your notebook some steps that you can take to show more clearly that life in Jesus Christ is a life of joy. Resolve to take those steps. Pray, asking God for help in this endeavor.

For Group Study

After studying the passage and discussing it, invite the group to try to see your church or community of faith as if they were outsiders looking in. When other people look at us, will they see joy or will they see bitterness? Will they see love or will they see rigidity?

Invite the group to make a list of the characteristics of your church that may attract outsiders, and another list of those other characteristics and practices that can drive away them. While remaining faithful to the gospel, what can we do so that outsiders may be attracted to our community of faith?

W E E K
SIX

First Day: Read Revelation 10:1-4

See: As in previous cases—for instance, when we thought that the end was at hand the moment the seventh trumpet had blown—our expectations are wrong. Once again John leaves us at the edge of our seats, awaiting the final outcome.

In this case, what interrupts our expectations is "another angel." We are told that it is "another" because it is not one of the seven angels with trumpets. The fact that it is described as a "mighty angel" leads some interpreters to think that it is Gabriel, whose name means "God is my strength." At any rate, this particular angel is described in majestic terms suggesting great stature ("wrapped in a cloud, with a rainbow over his head...his right foot on the sea and his left foot on the land"). This angel has a scroll. This is not the great scroll sealed with seven seals, but is much smaller and open. The day after tomorrow we shall return to this small book and its importance for John and his vision.

For the time being, John tells us that the angel shouted with a great voice, and that "the seven thunders sounded." But when John sought to write what he had heard, he was told: "Seal up what the seven thunders have said, and do not write it down."

Judge: There has been much debate about the meaning of these seven thunders and what they may have said. The one certain thing is that it is impossible to know. And that is not necessarily bad, because the voice kept John from writing what he had heard and therefore there is no point in our trying to discover or to guess what it could be.

What is clear is that there is a place in life for mystery and for the unknown. To be faithful and obedient, we do not have to know everything. We do not have to know what it was that the seven thunders said. Nor do we have to know, as some people seek to know, how and when the end of all times will come. What we have to know is what our responsibility is. The rest can easily turn into mere curiosity, and even into a kind of idolatry in which we imagine that, like God, we have to know every mystery.

It is very important to remember this, especially in our study of this book of Revelation. Many read as if it were a mine of hidden secrets where mysteries will be revealed—mysteries that otherwise they could not understand. But the fact is that in essence Revelation says the same thing as the rest of the New Testament: that the Lamb who was slain and yet lives must reign, and that those who are faithful will reign with him.

Act: Pray: I beseech you, my God and the God of John, that you teach me to read your Word, not as a matter of curiosity, seeking answers to unimportant questions, or to questions whose answers lie only in your hidden will, but seeking to discover what your will is for me. I beseech you to teach me to be obedient. Do not reveal all your mysteries to me. But do reveal what you want me to be in you. Amen.

Second Day: Read Revelation 10:5-7

See: Before continuing with the vision of the small scroll, John tells us that the angel swore a solemn oath—so solemn that it is made on behalf of God, "by him who lives forever and ever, who created heaven and what is in it, the earth and what is in it, and the sea and what is in it." The content of the oath is at the end of verse 6: "There will be no more delay." When reading these words (particularly in translations that say "there will be no more time"), it is necessary to clarify that this is not a philosophical statement, in the sense that when the purposes of God are fulfilled time will no longer exist. It is rather a final warning.

Much earlier, in Revelation 2:21, we were told that Jezebel had "time to repent." What the passage that we are studying now means is that there will no longer be time for repentance.

Judge: In a way, we come now to the highest level of warning: the warning that there will be no more warnings. The angel swears that the time for warnings is over. We must not imagine that because God has given warning after warning out of mercy, God will continue holding back the power of divine wrath and judgment.

One of the most insidious temptations for believers is to imagine that, because God is love and mercy, God's warnings will continue indefinitely, and we do not need to repent and to change our lives now since there will always be more warnings. But the truth is that the warnings of God will reach their limit, and, at that point, we shall have to face God's judgment or an incredulity and a disobedience such that they could not be moved even by the direst warnings.

Act: Are you one of those people who trust the mercy of God to such a point that you do not even try to be obedient? In such a case, consider the possibility that one day the angel of the Lord will tell you that there is no more time. Repent now. Ask now for forgiveness. Ask God for strength and guidance to continue living in holiness.

Third Day: Read Revelation 10:8-11

See: In contrast to the great scroll sealed with seven seals that passes directly from the hand of God to the Lamb, without even an angel touching it, this small scroll is given by the angel to John, with instructions to eat it. The passage is parallel to the call of Ezekiel, who also ingests a book. But, in contrast to the case of Ezekiel, for whom the book is "sweet as honey," for John the book is sweet to the palate but bitter to the stomach.

The text gives no further indication of what the content of this small scroll may have been. One may suppose that it is the message that John must proclaim. Once again, to be a prophet of God, John does not have to ingest the entire great scroll with the seven seals. He does not have to know the answer to all questions and to every mystery. All he needs is the small scroll with the message that God has entrusted to him. The great scroll with all its mysteries is the prerogative of God and the Lamb.

Why are we told that the book was bitter in John's stomach? A possibility is that it is made bitter by what is said in verse 11: that John must prophesy about many people, and nations, and languages, and kings. As we have seen, John was a Jew by birth, and the same was true of most of the members of the seven churches in Asia. But now he must announce a message that says that the love of God extends, not only to good and faithful Jews, but also to an entire variety of peoples. For a person raised in the traditions of Israel, such a message would be difficult and even bitter.

Judge: Once again we see that to be obedient it is not necessary to have the answer to all mysteries. John does not have to eat the whole scroll with seven seals. The smaller scroll suffices for him. Likewise, in order to be faithful, we today do not need to know exactly when or how the Lord will come. What is more, to insist too much on knowing such things, and to spend too much time trying to discover the answer, may well be an excuse for not being obedient in more immediate matters.

On the other hand, what we have seen about the bitter aftertaste of the small scroll is still true today. Today there are also many believers, sincere and devoted people, who nevertheless find it difficult to accept the fact that God loves and invites other people who are very different from them. That is what happens in some churches of the dominant culture when people of another culture begin to join them. Hispanics in the United States have frequently seen this. It is also what happens among some Hispanics with regard to people of another culture. The message that we must proclaim, even among our own people and culture, is "about many peoples and nations and languages and kings."

Consider the possibility, not only that your own presence may produce a bitter aftertaste for other people, but also that you may have the same attitude toward others. Thus, for instance, there are churches of the dominant culture that, even though they think they are open to others, are not in fact welcoming communities. And there are also Latino churches where most people are of a single national origin, and people of another nationality are not fully welcomed or given space and opportunity for growth and leadership. It is a common temptation for churches, no matter what their culture, race, or national origin, to find the inclusive message of John a bitter pill to swallow.

Act: Pray: Thank you, loving God, that you have included us among the many peoples, nations, and languages where your gospel has been preached. Help us accept those who represent other peoples, nations, and languages with a love similar to what you have shown us. Forgive our narrow vision and our prejudices. Help us love the entire world as you have loved us. Through Jesus Christ, your love made flesh. Amen.

Fourth Day: Read Revelation 11:1-2

See: After the vision of the angel with the small scroll, one would expect the blast of the final trumpet. Certainly, this must be the time. But there is still more to come, and John has another vision. Now he is given a measuring rod, and he is ordered to measure "the temple of God and the altar and those who worship there," but not to measure the court outside the temple.

The action of measuring is a sign of protection. When measuring the temple on behalf of God, what John is doing is claiming divine protection for that area. In not measuring the court of the Gentiles, he is leaving it at the mercy of the Gentiles. Thus, in all of Jerusalem the only area that is protected is the temple, its altar, and those who worship there. The rest will be given to destruction in such a way that the enemies "will trample over the holy city for forty-two months." Forty-two months are three and a half years. Since the number seven indicates fullness, the three and half years (a time that appears repeatedly in several different ways in the rest of the chapter) indicate a limited time—the opposite of seven years, which would denote an entire era.

Until Jerusalem was destroyed by the Romans in the year 70, the court of the Gentiles was reserved for those people who, although attracted by the faith of Israel, were not willing to become Jews. Thus the first thing this passage affirms is that those who are not willing to commit to God, no matter how "sympathetic" that may be, will not receive divine protection. They will be destroyed with the rest of the city.

We should also remember that John, and most Christians when Revelation was written, were Jews. Jerusalem and its temple had been destroyed little more than twenty-five years earlier. For these people, those events represented an inexplicable tragedy. The Holy City and its temple had been destroyed, and those who destroyed them were now masters of the world. The sad situation of the churches of Asia was due not only to the fact that they were small and persecuted, but also to the wider and painful reality that even the very symbol of biblical faith, the temple in Jerusalem, had been demolished and unbelievers now trampled the Holy Land.

In the context of such a situation, this vision tells John two things. It tells him first that although the physical temple has been destroyed, God protects God's people. This is the meaning of the action of measuring the temple, its altar, and those who worship in it. And the vision also tells John that the present condition of desolation, when the evil seem to lord it over the good, will come to an end, because its time is limited (forty-two months).

Judge: There are times when the church, and we as individuals, feel that the world is crashing down around us. This must have been the feeling of the churches in Asia when John wrote this vision. They were times of persecution and of apparent failure.

Have you lived through such times? Everything seems to turn out wrong. When we try to fix things, they actually get worse.

Sometimes it even seems that personal tragedies accumulate one on top of the other, and that God does not answer our prayers. If we have enemies, it seems that they are able to wrong us constantly and to go unpunished.

Has your church lived through such times? Resources are insufficient. A project that we undertook with much enthusiasm is defunct. Maybe the neighborhood where the church is has filled with hoodlums and exploiters who seem to undo whatever good the church can do. The budget does not allow us to do more. What is more, any drug pusher makes more money in a single day than the church can raise in an entire year. In such times, it seems that the enemy is more powerful than God.

When we find ourselves in such conditions, either at the personal level or as a church, this text tells us that those times will pass. Although for the time being it seems that nothing will be able to stop the power of evil and that things will continue worsening forever, the fact is that the evil may even trample the Holy City, but this will not last more than "forty-two months" (that is to say, a limited time).

Act: If you or your church are going through such difficult times, pray, requesting strength, faith, and patience to resist until the evil times pass. If not, know that such evil times will come, and prepare for them in prayer. Remember also that there are others who are themselves going through difficult times. Pray for them, that they may be comforted and that they may come to better times.

Fifth Day: Read Revelation 11:3-7

See: The two witnesses, two olive trees, or two lampstands are the two branches of the people of God: Israel and the church. Remember that in prophetic literature Israel is sometimes called an "olive tree" (Jeremiah 11:16; Hosea 14:6). These two witnesses are wearing sackcloth as a sign of repentance. Their message, the testimony that they must give, is a call to repentance.

The two witnesses have great power. Fire pours from their

mouths, and their enemies are destroyed. They have the power to shut the sky so that it does not rain (as Elijah did), or to transform the waters into blood (as in the time of Moses). Thus, the two olive trees seem to be indestructible.

But it is not so. They have been raised in order to provide a testimony. For that reason we are told that they have power to testify for 1,260 days (which is the same as 42 months, or three and a half years). The time of their power is limited, just as the time when evil reigns is limited. When they have completed their task, "the beast that comes up from the bottomless pit"— that is, Satan—will conquer and kill them.

Judge: Yesterday we centered our attention on the bad times, when we go through valleys of the shadow of death, when it seems that everything is stacked against us. We said that this happens to all of us, both as individuals and as the church. Today we see that there are times that seem to be just the opposite—times of victory and apparent power. According to the text, during those 1,260 days the two witnesses seem indestructible. But this is only because they have a testimony to give. Their apparent victory is fleeting.

This leads us to consider what may seem to be "good times" for the church and for believers. When things go well, we give thanks to God and we live under the illusion that all problems are past. There are churches that suddenly experience a great surge in strength and vitality. They grow quickly. They make plans for several projects at the same time, and they all yield positive results. Certainly it seems that God's favor is with them.

What is more, there are preachers who seem to imply that the reason their churches grow is that they are wise and faithful leaders. They claim that God makes the faithful to prosper and it is for that reason that they now are rich.

But it is necessary to be careful with such triumphalism. The two witnesses may seem powerful, yes; but God has put them there so that they may give a testimony for a limited time. Their apparent victory is as fleeting as that of the evil enemies who trampled the Holy City in yesterday's passage.

When we experience times of achievements and victories, it does not necessarily follow that we are more faithful than when we find ourselves in times of suffering and difficulties. Both good times and bad times are in the hands of God, and both will pass away.

Act: If you and your church are going through a period of achievements and victories, give thanks to God and ask God to prepare you for difficult times—that God will not allow you to get so used to victories and achievements that you come to think that when they are absent God too is absent. If, on the contrary, you and your church are going through times of difficulties, remember that those times are also finite and they too will pass.

Sixth Day: Read Revelation 11:8-10

See: The dead bodies of the two witnesses will be exposed in "the great city that is prophetically called Sodom and Egypt." To understand this, it is necessary to remember that in ancient times a "city" and a "state" were frequently the same thing. That is why here "Egypt" is the name of a "city." A "city" was not, as it is for us today, only an urban center, but was also all the territory that belonged to such a center and was governed from it. It is in that sense that Egypt is called a city.

The "great city" to which the text refers has two "prophetic" names, Sodom and Egypt. Sodom was a symbol of corruption. Egypt was a symbol of oppression because it was there that the people of Israel had to serve as slaves. Early Christians knew this "great city," which in fact is none other than Rome and its whole empire, by its corruption and oppression.

In other words, what John is saying is that the destruction of the "two witnesses"—Israel and the church—will take place openly in the Roman Empire. To understand this, it is necessary to remember that when Revelation was written both Judaism and Christianity were under enormous pressure, especially in the province of Asia. From the point of view of a Christian of Jewish origin, such as John, the Romans had set out to destroy the "two witnesses."

The death of these two witnesses will be publicly humiliating. This is what is meant by the statement that their bodies will be left unburied in the street of the great city. And also, people from all over the world will rejoice, since the witnesses had been "a torment" to them. This is to say that the witness of biblical faith is like a sting in the flesh of unbelievers, and that it is for that reason that the witnesses are persecuted.

What is more, those who will rejoice at the death of the two witnesses will not be only the Romans but also "members of the peoples and tribes and languages and nations." Just as the call of the Lamb is heeded and accepted by people of the most diverse races and cultures who will be in the presence of God and of the Lamb, so do those who oppose the Lamb and its followers represent all races and cultures.

Finally, note that this situation also lasts "three and a half days"—that is to say, a limited time.

Judge: Once again we are dealing with difficult times. Now they are so difficult that it seems that the final victory belongs to the beast from the bottomless pit. The two witnesses have died, and their bodies are subjected to jeers and insults.

But what probably most surprises us in this passage is that the enmity against the two witnesses is so widespread among all the nations, peoples, tribes, and languages. We sometimes think that what the church has to do is to gain greater popularity and acceptance in each culture. There is some truth in this, and it is for this reason that the Bible has been translated into so many languages, that we make an effort to use music that is compatible with each culture and situation, that we have youth camps, and so forth. But it is also true that when God's witnesses are faithful they have many enemies and that therefore popularity and acceptance cannot be the last measure for the faithfulness of a church.

What is more, when the church is truly faithful it inevitably makes enemies. If we preach against sin, we should not forget that there are in every society many persons who live by exploiting vices and sin. If we oppose injustice, we should not forget that in every unjust situation there is someone who benefits by that injustice and who therefore wants to see it continue. If God's witnesses are truly faithful, an unavoidable result will be that they will have enemies.

Another point that must be emphasized in this passage is that those who mock the two dead witnesses and rejoice over their death represent all races, nations, and cultures. The experience of minorities in the United States has frequently been one of oppression and exploitation on the part of some people of the dominant culture. As a reaction against that, many times we imagine that such exploitation is perpetrated only by people of that other culture. But at the same time we must take care lest we come to think that people of minority cultures are necessarily better or more faithful Christians than those of the dominant culture. There will be among all people some who will rejoice when learning of an occurrence like the death of the two witnesses.

Act: Evaluate the ministry and the activities of your church. Think not so much in terms of success as in terms of fidelity. Is your church faithful in the proclamation of the message of salvation? Is it faithful in denouncing the injustices that exist in the surrounding society? Is it faithful in proclaiming and being a demonstration of a new reign of peace, justice, and love? What enemies has your church gained due to its faithfulness? Write down your reflections and share them with other members of your church.

Seventh Day: Read Revelation 11:11-14

See: Once again, the time of the apparent victory of the beast is finite (which is symbolized by "three and a half days"). After that time, the two prophets are vindicated. God restores to them the spirit of life, and they arise.

The vindication of the two witnesses is total. Those who mocked their bodies are now terrified, as the loud voice from heaven summons the two witnesses and they ascend in a cloud. Those who had earlier tormented the two witnesses now witness their vindication. That victory includes being taken up to heaven, where one may suppose (although the text does not say so) that they will live eternally.

Meanwhile, on the earth there is a great earthquake that destroys a tenth of the city and kills seven thousand people. Once again, that number should not be taken literally. If the number seven is a sign of fullness, the number 7,000 indicates a huge mortality rate.

Now, finally, after so many warnings, John tells us that "the rest were terrified and gave glory to the God of heaven."

Verse 14 declares that this earthquake is the second woe and that the third is still pending. It is interesting to notice that in the case of the seals and the trumpets the first few in each series take up little space and each seal or trumpet is treated more extensively than the previous one; but in the case of the woes the first one is very extensive, and of the second all that is said is what we read in verse 13. As for the third, quite surprisingly, nowhere in the rest of the book are we told that *this is the third woe*.

There are several ways to explain this. Possibly the third woe is the final judgment that comes at the blast of the seventh trumpet. In that case, it is significant to note that, as we shall see tomorrow, what follows after that trumpet is a vision of joy and celebration; and, although we are told that God's enemies have been conquered, nothing is said about their punishment. Perhaps this is the worst woe: that the condemned are not even mentioned but are totally forgotten.

According to another interpretation, the third woe is the series of cups of wrath that appear later in the book. The difficulty with this interpretation is that it does not explain why the book never says that this is the third woe, and also that such a woe, rather than a single event as in the two previous cases, is an entire series of further tribulations or woes.

Thus, the safest option may be simply to say that John does not mention the third woe. This remains as one more warning that in spite of the terrible events that are described in the book, the final one, the final condemnation, is worse yet.

Judge: In each of the last four days we have seen the people of God in different circumstances. First (the fourth day) they were persecuted and oppressed, and maybe perplexed before the destruction of some of their dreams and dearest symbols (in that case, Jerusalem and its temple). Then (the fifth day) they were victorious and apparently invincible, presenting a powerful and unrestrained testimony. Then (yesterday) we saw them apparently destroyed, subjected to the jeers of their enemies. Last (today) we have seen them in their final victory.

Maybe the most important thing for us today is to determine in which of those different circumstances the church finds itself. Certainly, we are not in the fourth, for we still await the day of the final consummation. But in which of the other three are we?

When asking this question, the first thing we have to understand is that none of those conditions is worthier than the other two. All are conditions through which the church has had to pass at one time or another. And each has its own dangers and temptations.

First there are churches that are oppressed and persecuted. Although today in most countries there is no persecution like those in times of the Roman Empire, there are indeed places where Christianity is still persecuted or where particular church traditions are suppressed. Until fairly recently, in some countries of Latin America, Protestants suffered persecution, and many gave witness to their faith by giving their lives for it. In large sections of Sudan, Nigeria, and several other countries, Christians are being persecuted right now.

But perhaps we do not need to go so far to find churches in difficult situations. In some of the Hispanic neighborhoods in the United States, churches live under conditions similar to those we have studied for three days. Their buildings, when there are any, have broken windowpanes and frequently obscenities are written on the walls. In those neighborhoods those in practical authority are often hoodlums and drug pushers, and Christian young people are frequently oppressed by their peers and by the gangs to which those peers belong. Some churches do not dare have worship in the evenings for fear of crime. To be a believer in such circumstances is very similar to being a believer in the circumstances that are described in Revelation 11:1-2. In such cases, it is important to remember that such circumstances last but a limited time (what Revelation calls 42 months).

On the other hand, there are churches that seem to have an overwhelming strength. Their worship services are filled to capacity, and every day there seem to be more people attending worship. The enthusiasm in such churches is such that nothing seems to be able to stop them. They are like the "two witnesses" in Revelation during their time of success. Yet, it is important for such churches to remember that their success will also last only for a limited period (1,260 days = 42 months).

Finally, there are places where it seems that the church has died. Ancient buildings are now empty. Sometimes this is the result of persecution, and in other cases it is simply the result of lack of interest on the part of former believers. For a while it was thought that Christianity had disappeared in China. But when circumstances changed, it was discovered that there were still millions of Christians in the country. In many countries of Europe, although there are big and beautiful buildings, there is hardly a church because very few people attend worship anymore. But neither of those situations will last forever. As Revelation says, they will last "three and half days."

Possibly your church finds itself in one of these situations in some respect, and in another situation in a different respect. For example, it is possible that your denomination has prestige at the national level, but that in the neighborhood where your local church is located the situation is very different. What we must do is examine the life of our church to see which of these situations best describes us, in order then to decide what it is that we must do.

Act: Talk with other people in your church about how and to what extent your church is faithful to the gospel. In what situation do we find ourselves? Are we in a situation of oppression or of privilege? In that situation, what should we do to be more obedient? Is there in your church an organized group for studying

the Bible and for discussing matters such as these? If not, talk to
your pastor so that one may be set up.

For Group Study

Divide the group in two. The first one should try to imagine
what Christian life would be like in the difficult circumstances
that are described in verses 1 and 2. This group can make use of
all they have learned during these weeks of Bible study. The second group should imagine what Christian life would be like if
the church had the sort of success that is described in verses 3-6.
After giving them some minutes for discussion, gather to the
two groups and have each one report on its conversation.

Then lead a discussion, asking to what extent your present situation is similar to or different from those described in
Revelation.

W E E K
SEVEN

First Day: Read Revelation 11:15-17

See: After a long wait, we finally come to the seventh trumpet. Remember that the seven trumpets are what appear with the opening of the seventh seal and that therefore it seems that the end is, so to speak, just around the corner.

What the seventh trumpet seems to call forth is a great celestial act of praise. In the previous trumpets, although what John sees takes place in heaven, he is also shown what happens on the earth, the great evils that are unleashed upon the earth. After this seventh trumpet, John focuses his attention on the celestial liturgy, on the worship that is rendered to God upon the announcement of the final victory.

In that worship, "loud voices" announce that victory, declaring that "the kingdom of the world has become the kingdom of our Lord and of his Messiah, and he will reign forever and ever." Remember that the one writing these words, the ones who first read them aloud in the churches, and those who first heard their reading, were all subjects of the powerful Roman Empire. To write, to say, or to listen to such words could well be interpreted as a treasonable act, because what was being said was that the day would come when all kingdoms, including Rome, would be in the hands of God. In brief, the end of all human kingdoms was being announced, but very particularly and concretely the end of the Roman Empire!

In verse 16, as in several previous cases, John tells us that the twenty-four elders respond to all this with words and gestures of adoration and of gratitude. Notice that the elders give thanks that God has reclaimed God's great power. The significance of this becomes clear if we remember that the twenty-four elders represent the entire people of God—that is to say, both Israel and the church. These people have suffered repeatedly at the hands of tyrants and of powerful rulers. Many have suffered torture and death. Others have suffered vituperation and scorn. Many have suffered oppression and exploitation. But now God has finally claimed God's great power, and all those powers of oppression, persecution and exploitation have been dethroned.

Judge: How often have you heard that the church should not get involved in politics? If that is the case, how can one explain this passage, which would necessarily have subversive undertones in times of the Roman Empire (or of any other empire)? Could it be that the Christian message is in itself subversive, and that those who claim it is not are in fact preaching a partial message? Consider what this may imply. The Christian message affirms in the first place that the purpose of life cannot be in any of the fleeting things that this life can provide—material goods, pleasures, and fame. These can be either good or evil, but they are never enough to bring true happiness. But the fact is that a goodly part of the current economy is built on the myth that if we possess this or that it will make us happy. That is what we are repeatedly told in advertisements in the media. Practically from the day of our birth, we are led to think that if we buy and we have a particular toy, we will be happy. Since the Christian message claims that this is false, that message is subversive of the present economic order.

Something similar happens in the political arena. Throughout history, those who rule have always sought to appear to be perfectly wise and just. In every country a nationalist patriotism is promoted that tries to convince everyone that this particular country is the best in the world, its flag the most beautiful of all, and its language the most expressive. That nationalism is sometimes promoted by means of campaigns against the nation's rivals, real or imagined. (Remember, for instance, the pervading atmosphere during the years of the Cold War.) All of this is then used to bolster the authority of governments and national rulers.

But the Christian message affirms that all these "kingdoms"—which also include republics—are bound to disappear and that in the end there is only one King or government that really counts. That is certainly subversive. And it will become even more subversive of those states that have a higher notion of their own authority.

How, then, can anyone claim that the church should have nothing to do with politics? Would it be more exact to say that the church should practice and announce a politics that affirms that there is no other Lord but God, and that all other rulers deserve only a conditional obedience, limited by what we know to be God's will of love and justice?

Act: Look again at your political commitments. If you belong to a particular party, make sure your loyalty to that party does not lead you to actions and attitudes contrary to your loyalty to God. If you do not belong to any party, consider how you may participate in political life and give witness to the will of God. Write down your reflections. If there are other people in your church or community of faith following this study, compare your notes with theirs.

Second Day: Read Revelation 11:18-19

See: The twenty-four elders continue praising and thanking God for God's great victory. As they say, "the nations raged." But against them the wrath of God has come, and the time has come to reward those who have been faithful and to destroy those who destroyed the earth.

Notice that those who are to be destroyed will be punished, not only because they persecuted the people of God but also because they destroyed the earth. The punishment of God comes not only to vindicate God's people but also to vindicate all of God's creation that the destroyers have exploited and destroyed. Revelation is not only about the final victory of Christians, but also and primarily about the final victory of God, which is also the victory of the whole creation, until then subject to powers of evil.

The vision finishes with an announcement of the final presence of God among God's people. This is what is meant by saying that the temple in heaven was open and that the ark of the covenant was in the temple. The old ark of the covenant was lost, and there were many legends about what had become of it. There was a Jewish tradition that when the purposes of God were fulfilled and Israel was completely restored, the ark would return to the temple. There was also a tradition that the temple of Jerusalem was but an imitation of the true temple of God in heaven. What John is saying is that now all this has been completed. The temple in heaven is open and the ark is in it. God is with the people, and God's reign shall have no end.

Judge: The reference to "those that destroy the earth" should make us think. It is not necessary to be very up to date with the news to know to what extent human beings, and mainly modern civilization, have destroyed the earth. There are lakes that used to be great seas, where now nothing can live. There are rivers so polluted that sometimes they will even catch fire. The forests of the Amazon and of the Congo are disappearing quickly. Those of Europe and of China are long gone. The air of some cities is so polluted that it is dangerous to breathe. High above us, the ozone layer that protects all of life seems to be threatened. Every day several animal species become extinct. And the justification for much of this destruction is that some people will be more comfortable, that there may be more automobiles, that there may be recreation areas and resorts, that fuel may be cheaper, and so on.

Could it be that, either by our actions or by our inactions, many of us should be counted among "those who destroy the earth"?

Act: Talk to others in church and in your place of work about "these matters" using materials that cause less environmental damage. Insist on conserving energy. Find out what groups in your community or nation are devoted to protecting the environment and offer them your support and participation. Teach your children about environmental pollution and why it is necessary to conserve and to protect the resources of nature.

Third Day: Read Revelation 12:1-2

See: When we come to chapter 12 of Revelation it seems that we enter new territory. Notice that John does not say that this is the continuation of the same vision he has been describing so far. In chapter 12, he does not say that he had a vision, but simply that a sign appeared in heaven. Thus it is quite possible that the vision that inspired the beginning of the book ends with chapter 11 and that what follows is a series of independent visions. It is important to take this possibility into account, so as not to read the entire book as if it were a single vision or a program or chronological plan for the last times. What is said in chapter 12, for instance, seems to refer to events previous to what is announced in chapter 11. (In chapter 11 the last trumpet is announced, and now in 12 we are back to the Messiah's birth.)

Who is this woman "clothed with the sun, with the moon under her feet, and on her head a crown of twelve stars"? The Catholic tradition has usually understood this to refer to the Virgin Mary, and therefore many famous paintings depict Mary standing on the moon with twelve stars around her head. But most probably the vision refers to the people of God as a whole—to Israel, to the church, and in a way also to Mary, who is the physical link between Israel and the church. This woman is pregnant and about to give birth—a metaphor that can be applied equally to Israel, to Mary, and to the church.

Judge: Since we now enter a second part of Revelation, this may be a good moment to review what we have seen up to this point and how it relates to the passage about the woman clothed with the sun. As we have seen repeatedly, in Revelation the people of God includes both Israel and the church. That is the symbolism of the twenty-four elders. This is why John speaks, on the one hand, of a great multitude of 144,000 from the twelve tribes of Israel, and, on the other, of a multitude from all peoples, nations, and tongues.

This symbolism is important, because if we forget it we run the risk of thinking that the redeeming plan of God begins with the birth of Jesus. It is not so. The redeeming plan of God is set in motion from the beginning of creation. It is for that reason that the Christian Bible contains not only the Christian books that today form the New Testament, but also the Jewish books that today Christians call the Old Testament.

Act: Pray, giving thanks to God, not only for Jesus and his gospel but also for all that God has done for the redemption of the world through Israel. Discuss this with other people in your church.

Fourth Day: Read Revelation 12:3-5

See: Here the dragon appears for the first time in Revelation. It is described as being red, with seven heads, ten horns, and seven diadems.

Throughout Christian history, there have been many attempts to determine the exact meaning of each of these heads, horns, and diadems. Some have claimed that the seven heads are seven kings and have given them names. Others have tried to explain how it is possible for seven heads to have ten horns, and have wondered if the three extra horns were all on the same head or on several.

Such explanations are nonsense. The vision is not a symbolic representation of all of history, in which each head or each diadem has to correspond to king so-and-so or to a particular country (usually, in the case of most of these interpreters, a country we do not like). Once again, the numbers seven and ten are a sign of fullness. The horn is a symbol of power, the head a symbol of authority, and the diadem of government. Thus, all that this imagery intends to claim is that the dragon holds all the power, all the authority, and all the governments on earth. Its red color, the color of blood, indicates that all this power is in the service of death and violence.

The dragon is so enormous that at a single sweep of its tail, a third of the stars drop to earth. This huge dragon is standing in front of the woman, waiting for the birth of her child in order to devour it. But when the child is born, God protects it by snatching it away.

Finally, the text tells us that this child of the woman clothed in the sun will "rule all the nations with a rod of iron."

Judge: There are many possible interpretations of this passage—all very interesting, but many lacking much grounding on the text itself. What interests us here is the immense power of evil. One of the reasons evil often surprises us and is able to conquer us is that we do not realize how powerful it really is. We sometimes imagine that evil is little more than a bad decision that we make and that therefore we can overcome it by simply making good decisions. But evil is much more than that. Evil is the sum of all the wrong that humans do and think, and still more.

Evil has power. In this text, it is painted as a great dragon that has the fullness of power and of authority. This is nothing to scoff at. And its purpose is to devour and destroy the Son who will rule the world. In other words, what Revelation suggests is a great cosmic drama in which the Evil One opposes the plans of God, and does everything possible to destroy those plans.

Do you believe that if we took evil more seriously we would know better how to defend ourselves against it? Could it be that evil sometimes catches us unawares, because we do not realize the full extent of its power and therefore think we can deal with it without God's help?

Act: Think about evil in your own community. Try to see it not as a series of events or disconnected ills, but rather as an organized system. For instance, if the most visible ill in your community is alcoholism, do not stop at saying so. Consider who benefits from the sale and consumption of alcohol. Consider who provides support to those people and companies that benefit from the inordinate consumption of alcohol, and why. Consider how much influence those people who benefit from the use of the alcohol have in governmental circles. In other words, try to see evil as a whole and to analyze its connections and systems of support. Then begin talking to others in order to make plans to confront and oppose evil.

Fifth Day: Read Revelation 12:6

See: What we read yesterday, that the woman's son was snatched and taken away to God and to God's throne so the dragon could not devour it, probably refers to the cross and resurrection of Jesus. The dragon awaited his birth to destroy him, and he thought he had achieved this in the crucifixion; but on the third day God gave the victory to the Son who was snatched to heaven and to the very throne of God.

This, however, leaves the woman on earth. God's people have given birth to the victorious Messiah; but they must still live on earth, where the dragon seeks revenge against them.

This is why the woman flees to the wilderness, where a place has been prepared for her by God. In John's time, particularly in the province of Asia and its surroundings, both Israel and the church faced difficulties and even persecution. There was very little they could do to avoid those difficulties. The only road left to them was to remain firm in their faith while waiting for better times. In a way, this experience was parallel to that of Israel in the desert, waiting for the day when it could settle in the promised land.

Once again, as in the previous chapter, the text indicates that this condition of refuge in the desert is not permanent but rather will last a limited time (1,260 days = 42 months = three and a half years).

Judge: Think of your own church or community of faith. Is it in some sense living "in the desert"? It is clear that, until the final day, the whole church lives as in the desert, while waiting for the promised land. But there are moments when the church lives more clearly in the desert. For example, when Protestants were persecuted in France and had to meet in secret, they began calling themselves "the church of the desert."

Back to your church, what deserts is it crossing? Some churches, for instance, do not have a place to meet. In some denominations, ethnic minority churches feel marginalized and sometimes find it difficult for their concerns to be heard by the denomination as a whole. Or perhaps your church is in a neighborhood where violence is constant and the church and its members suffer from it.

Remember that in the passage that we are studying, it is God who takes the woman to the desert to protect her from the dragon. Could it be that some of the difficulties we are facing are actually protecting us from temptations that would possibly destroy us?

Act: Write down your reflections on the question just posed. What temptations would success bring about? With the help of those reflections, consider what steps must be taken so that when circumstances change and become more favorable, the church is ready to respond without succumbing to the temptations of success.

(Remember that the woman will be in the desert a limited time. The present difficulties will pass. Get ready, and help the church get ready, for the future.)

Sixth Day: Read Revelation 12:7-9

See: The passage may surprise us, because it speaks of a great war in heaven. The idea that we generally hold of heaven depicts it as a peaceful place, where everything and all obey God. Although frequently we say that Satan is a fallen angel, we usually understand this to mean that he has been expelled from heaven from the very moment of his fall. But that is not what this text indicates. The battle between "Michael and his angels" on one hand, and "the dragon and his angels" on the other, takes place in heaven. Until that moment, Satan and his angels have not been expelled from heaven. Note that this expulsion takes place only after the Messiah's victory. Indeed, in some translations verse 7 begins with the word "then." The battle

takes place as a result of the birth of the Messiah, and its outcome is the expulsion of the dragon and his angels from heaven
to earth. Until then, there was "place for them in heaven." It is
when explaining the result of the battle, in verse 9, that the text
tells us that the dragon is none other than the Devil, Satan, or
"that ancient serpent."

Judge: What all this means for us is that the drama of redemption
is much wider in scope than we often imagine. In general, when
speaking of the cross of Christ, we think only in terms of our own
sin and how by means of the cross we are redeemed from it. But
redemption is much more than that. According to this passage,
what Jesus Christ has achieved in the cross is not only our personal redemption, but also the final victory over Satan and his legions.
It is because the One who was born from the woman clothed in the
sun has conquered the dragon and has been snatched to heaven
that Michael and his angels now can expel Satan and his legions.

This is another way of saying what we saw previously, that
the Lamb that has been slaughtered is the only one able to open
the seven seals. It is due to his victory, to his cross and resurrection, that the Lamb can open the seals. Thus, the victory that
takes place on earth also unleashes the events in heaven that
John now describes.

Could it be that our vision of Jesus Christ and his saving work
is too narrow?

Act: Pause to consider the vision you have of Jesus Christ and of
what he has achieved through the cross and the resurrection. If
that vision is limited to saving you and others, you have not yet
captured the cosmic vision—the victory of Christ—that
Revelation proclaims. Review what we have studied, remembering that all that is said under the heading of the seven seals has
been made possible only because of the death and resurrection
of Jesus Christ. (Remember that the Lamb who was slaughtered
is the only one who has the power to open the seals.) Try to
think of the victory of Jesus Christ in cosmic terms. This is a victory over all the powers of evil. Write down your reflections.

Seventh Day: Read Revelation 12:10-17

See: The loud voice in heaven explains what has happened. Finally ("now") "the salvation and the power" of God and of Christ have been affirmed. This has taken place because "the accuser of our comrades"—that is to say, the dragon or Satan—has finally been expelled from heaven. Calling Satan "the accuser" has a long history in the religion of Israel. Remember, for instance, the beginning of the book of Job, where it is Satan who accuses Job of not being truly just or at least of not being just in such a way that he can stand strong in the face of adversity.

Notice that the victory belongs not only to Christ, or to Michael and his angels, but also to believers on earth, whom the voice in heaven calls "our comrades." In verse 11 we are told that "they have conquered him by the blood of the Lamb and by the word of their testimony, for they did not cling to life even in the face of death."

In other words, the struggle of the faithful on earth against their persecutors is a struggle against Satan, and when they conquer by remaining faithful, that victory resounds even in heaven.

Then comes verse 12, which places the entire situation in a new light. According to what is said there, the result of the defeat of Satan and his angels in heaven is an even more difficult struggle on earth. Having been expelled from heaven, and aware that his time is short, Satan unleashes his anger with more furor on the earth. Or, as verse 13 says, precisely because he has been expelled from heaven, the dragon now persecutes the woman clothed in the sun with even greater fury.

We thus return to what was said previously about the woman finding refuge in the desert for a limited time. ("A time, and times, and half a time" is three and a half times [1 + 2 + ½ = 3½], that is to say, a limited time, half of seven times.) This shows once again that Revelation is not a chronology or a program of the final events. Here, for instance, we are back to the time of the persecution of the church, even though in earlier passages it would seem that such a time has already passed.

In his intent to persecute the woman, Satan is frustrated once again, for even the earth comes to the aid of the woman. This enrages Satan even more, and he goes off "to make war on the rest of her children, those who keep the commandments of God and hold the testimony of Jesus."

Judge: The most common way to explain the sufferings of the faithful is that it is a punishment of God. It was thus that Job's friends tried to explain his sufferings. Job's answer, refusing to accept such an explanation, was correct. But although we know Job's friends' explanation is not correct, it still nags us, and we easily fall back on it when we find ourselves suffering or in difficulties.

Sometimes a similar explanation is offered indirectly. Such is the case, for instance, of the "gospel of prosperity" that has become so popular in some circles. According to that theology, the prosperity of individuals is in direct relationship to their fidelity. If you are faithful, we are told, you will have money, health, success, happiness, fame. The logical conclusion is that those who are poor, ill, or unsuccessful have been less than faithful and that their difficulties are of their own making.

Revelation flatly denies that sort of theology. If that theology were correct, we would have to say that the church of Laodicea was more faithful than the church of Smyrna, when in fact it was just the opposite. The church of Laodicea, rich and prosperous, was less faithful than that of Smyrna, which was poor and persecuted.

Another common explanation is simply that in life there are always afflictions and difficulties. If something negative happens to us, that is simply part of the natural rhythm of life. If that explanation is correct, all we can do is to avoid difficulties and try to live as comfortably and peacefully as we can, until death frees us from this vale of sorrow.

But that too is not the explanation of Revelation. Or, rather, that is not the whole explanation. Certainly, life always brings its sufferings. But Revelation sees the sufferings and the temptations of the faithful in a different light: they are due partly at least— and no matter how strange that may seem to us—to Satan's defeat! What the faithful suffer is not just the normal measure of difficulties in life. It is actually the result of a last- minute resistance of an evil that is already defeated. Its fury is the fury of those who have already lost the battle and lash wildly about.

The significance of this is that when the faithful understand their sufferings and difficulties in this way, they will understand that it is not always good or wise to flee from them. If the evil that we suffer is due only to the nature of life, the wisest thing is to avoid it whenever we can. But if that evil is due in part to the fact that our enemy is already conquered, then that evil becomes a test of our faithfulness, and in some cases we will have to face it with valiant firmness rather than fleeing from it.

Such was the case of those persecuted churches in the province of Asia. If they saw the pressure on the part of the state and society as simply one of the normal pains of life, they could easily have succumbed to that pressure. But if they understood it as part of a great battle in which their calling was to stand firm until the final victory, they could remain faithful until the time of that victory.

Do we ever find ourselves in a similar situation? Could it be that we sometimes succumb before temptation because we do not even recognize it as such? We convince ourselves that what we should do is look for the easiest and most comfortable life possible, and the result is that we allow ourselves to be carried away by all sorts of temptations.

Act: Think of some important decision that you have had to make recently. It could be, for instance, a decision about your career or work, or your relationship with somebody, or how to respond to somebody who mistreated you. In that decision, did you think only of what would be best and easiest for you? Did you consider the possibility that the easy solution may in fact have been a temptation calling you away from your duty? Take some time to consider this.

Write down your reflections. If you come to the conclusion that you made a bad decision, consider how and to what extent you can correct it.

For Group Study

Review the entire chapter 12 of Revelation. Before the session, ask two or three people to prepare a presentation before the entire group. They should imagine that they are members of the church of Smyrna and that they have just listened to the reading of chapter 12. Then they should have a conversation among themselves, commenting on the thoughts that the whole chapter has evoked in them.

After that conversation, lead the group in a similar discussion.

Finally, ask what thoughts this entire conversation evokes in them as they seek to be faithful Christians in the twenty-first century.

W E E K

EIGHT

First Day: Read Revelation 13:1-4

See: The chapter opens with John standing on the sand of the sea. (Since it is possible to translate that first sentence in the sense that it was the dragon that stood on the sand, some versions translate the passage in that way. In that case they count this sentence as verse 18 of the previous chapter.) What follows seems not to be a continuation of the previous vision, but the report of a separate vision.

Starting from this point, some of John's visions will have stronger political connotations than the ones studied up to now, and this is one of the reasons the book uses symbolic language— so that those who were not believers and familiar with the Bible could not easily understand.

John sees a beast coming out of the sea. This beast resembles much that was said earlier about the dragon, for it too has seven heads and ten horns. Its body is a combination of the beasts of Daniel's vision (Daniel 7:3-7) that in the book of Daniel represented the empires of the time. Thus this beast in Revelation represents the great Roman Empire, the epitome and culmination of all previous empires.

It is for this reason that the beast is said to come out of the sea. Remember that from the point of view of Asia Minor or of Patmos, the Romans came from the west, over the sea. It was mainly by sea that the new governors and other officials coming from Rome arrived in Asia Minor. Thus, the beast that comes out of the sea in whose heads and horns seem to reside the fullness of power and whose body summarizes all the empires of the earth, is the Roman Empire.

John does not mince words: it is the dragon that has given power to the beast. This does not mean that political powers are always bad. But, at least in this case, the power of the beast comes from the support of the dragon.

The result is that the whole earth marvels, and they adore the dragon and the beast, telling themselves that nothing and nobody can ever have greater power than they do.

(There has been much discussion about the meaning of the head with a "mortal wound" that had been healed. Some suggest that it is a reference to a legend of the time, according to which Nero would return to life. The most probable is that it is a way of imitating or counterfeiting the Lamb that was slaughtered, and yet lives. In other words, that the beast is a parody, a bad imitation, of the Lamb.)

Judge: Most Christians today (or at least, most of those who will read this book) do not have to face an empire whose blasphemy reaches the level of the claims of the Roman Empire, whose emperors claimed to be divine and demanded worship. But we will still have to face many powerful and prestigious enemies.

One of those enemies, for instance, may be the very culture in which we live, which claims that the value of persons depends on what they consume, on what they spend, on what they buy, or on what they have. On television there are many very popular programs that describe and extol the life of the rich and powerful. The power of that culture is such that it penetrates our homes and even our consciences. Will we have the valor to give such things the name they deserve, of satanic beasts?

Another of those enemies may be a social order such that almost as a matter of policy many people are excluded. That was one of the Roman government's main problems in the province of Asia, where, as we have seen, the price of bread had risen to such a point that the poor did not have enough to eat. Does the same thing happen in some of our countries, even in spite of all our prosperity, technical advances, tall buildings, modern highways, and so forth? Will we have the courage to point out that there is also misery, injustice, and hunger?

Continue reflecting along those lines, and you will see that there are many enemies that confront us with situations and alternatives similar to those that the beast that came out of the sea placed before the first readers of Revelation.

Act: Focus your attention on one of the enemies mentioned above, or on another that you have discovered in your own reflection. Consider how that enemy tries to force you to give in, and to abandon your principles and your Christian commitment. Determine the strategy that you will follow in order to stand firm against those temptations.

Second Day: Read Revelation 13:5-8

See: The meaning of these verses should be clear. In the first place, the beast has authority for a limited period (the forty-two months or three and a half years that we have seen repeatedly). Second, the beast speaks blasphemies against God and against all that has to do with God. Third, the beast has power to conquer the saints—that is to say, the believers. Finally, it has "authority over every tribe and people and language and nation."

Since the beast from the sea represents the Roman Empire, the passage is saying what all know: that the power of that empire seems to reach the entire world. (Although at the time it was known that there were other territories beyond the borders of the Roman Empire, the attitude of Rome was that the rest of the world was not even worthy of mention. The entire "civilized" world was supposedly part of the Roman Empire. Although this was not true, it certainly was the prevailing attitude in Rome.)

The passage also says about the Roman Empire what believers in Asia already know: that it speaks blasphemies against God and that it has the power to destroy the faithful. On the first point, the titles that the emperors were given were sufficient proof (titles such as "Lord and God"). On the second, the proof was unnecessary, for already Christians had suffered under the power of the Empire.

What the text adds, and would be seen as a subversive message by the authorities had they heard it, is that the power of this apparently omnipotent beast will last only for a limited time (the three and a half symbolic years that we have found repeatedly in our study of Revelation).

Judge: Exiled on a very small island by order of the most powerful empire that the region had ever seen, John dares to say that the power of that empire is limited. He has no illusions about the Roman Empire. He does not deny the blasphemies it promotes. He does not deny that for the time being it has the power to destroy the faithful. He simply reminds his readers that it is not eternal. He places the Roman Empire where it properly belongs. He challenges its claim to ultimate and everlasting power. He reminds his readers that, no matter how very powerful the Empire might seem for the time being, in the end it too will fall.

Do we have the faith to say the same with regard to the beasts that today oppose the will of God? When some enemy seems terribly powerful, do we remember that its power will not last more than the forty-two symbolic months—that is to say, a limited time?

Think again about some of the enemies that were mentioned in yesterday's study, or of which you thought. Do you have full confidence that this enemy is not eternal, that its hour will come, just as it arrived for the Roman Empire?

Without that conviction, the church and its members fall prey to fear of the future. With it, they will face the morrow with the certainty that the future belongs to God and to God's followers. That is the heart of the message of Revelation.

Act: Repeat again and again that the future belongs only to God. Think of each of the enemies of the faith that came to mind yesterday. Say to them: "I will not fear your power, because it will pass. The only power that will not pass is the power of God." Consider what this implies for the way you must face your enemies and temptations. Write down your reflections.

Third Day: Read Revelation 13:9-10

See: After the vision of the beast from the sea, John finishes this section with a warning that reminds us of the end of each of the seven letters at the beginning of the book: "Let anyone who has an ear listen." What this means is that nobody has an excuse, because all have been given the opportunity to heed the warning.

Then follows a small poem. In the English translation one does not notice that it is poetry; but this is quite clear in the original Greek. The poem is a quotation of some phrases that appear twice in the book of Jeremiah. The first time they appear (Jeremiah 15:2) they are a warning to the Hebrew people before the exile, warning them of the destruction that must come to Jerusalem. The second time (Jeremiah 43:11) they are a warning to those who had taken refuge in Egypt, disobeying the divine command. Egypt, just like Jerusalem, would be destroyed by the Babylonians. When mentioning this passage, John is reminding his readers that disobedience has unavoidable consequences and that nobody can hide from them.

Judge: The obedience that God required of the people of Judea in times of Jeremiah seemed too harsh and therefore they tried to evade the divine demand, but they were not successful. The obedience that God required of the church in the time of John was equally hard, and for that reason John reminds his readers that it is impossible to hide from the consequences of disobedience.

Could it be that we sometimes try to hide from God when we find the obedience that God requires of us too difficult or too costly? We are quite willing to be counted among the believers when it is only a matter of attending worship and making an offering. But when we begin to study the Word of God, and we see that the obedience that is required of us has to do with the way we relate to each other, with the way we spend our money, with the way we invest our time, with the way we earn our living, in short, with everything, we find the price too high and we try to hide from that sort of obedience.

We hide by looking for an easier sort of Christianity. We hide behind the excuse that the options are not clear and that therefore we do not know what we must do. We hide behind the myth that the Christian faith has nothing to do with politics or with the economy or with the social order. We hide in a thousand ways. But God will find us.

Act: Write the following in your notebook:

Lord, forgive me for trying to hide from a full obedience to you. When you have called me to _____ *[fill the blanks with whatever fits your own story],* I _____. Give me the faith and the courage to be faithful and obedient. By Jesus Christ who was obedient until death, and death on a cross. Amen.

Fourth Day: Read Revelation 13:11-15

See: Now another beast appears on the scene. This one comes from the earth. If the beast that comes from the sea refers to Roman might, the beast that comes from the earth probably refers to local authorities, both political and religious, that pay homage to Rome. To understand this it is necessary to remember that most of Asia was not conquered militarily by Rome. Rather, it was the leading social classes of that region—in some cases the local kings and in others the priests and the political leaders—who made alliances with Rome and eventually surrendered their territories to the Roman Empire. In most of the cases, the Romans did not depose those authorities but rather placed them under their rule, as instruments to enforce the will of Rome.

That relationship between local and Roman authorities is described in the relationship between the beast that comes from the sea and the beast that comes from the earth. The latter promotes the authority of the first and even deifies it. This describes the relationship that in fact existed between the Roman authorities and those of Asia. For instance, in several of the main cities of Asia, temples were erected to the goddess Rome or to the

Emperor, and this was done at the direction, not of the Roman authorities as such, but of the local aristocracy. (Some interpreters suggest that verse 15 refers to a trick on the part of the local priests by which they gave speech to the images of the gods, including the goddess Rome.) As an indication that those authorities seek to pass themselves off as legitimate and as defenders of the people, the text tells us that this beast, although it looks like a lamb, in fact speaks as a dragon. It seems to be on the side of the Lamb, but it serves Satan.

Judge: Something similar often happens today both at the international level and at the local. At the international level, the exploitation of the poorest countries by the richest ones takes place with the acquiescence and support of the rich classes in the exploited countries.

At the local level, in many of our neighborhoods poverty becomes worse because a good part of the resources of the people will end up in the hands of absent exploiters who get rich by legal means such as excessive rents, and by illegal means such as the sale of drugs. But whether their methods are legal or illegal, such exploiters always have people from the neighborhood who are their representatives and agents and who in exchange receive a small portion of the power that the absentee exploiters have, and of the economic resources they take from the people. And, today as then, many times those elements insist that they are from the neighborhood, even though in fact they serve the interests of others—they appear to be lambs, but in fact they serve the dragon.

If the church of Revelation was aware of such situations, should we not seek a similar awareness?

Act: Choose any one of the many channels that are used to siphon resources from our poorer neighborhoods—for example, the sale of alcohol, the sale of drugs, usury, uninhabitable rental properties, gambling. In the case of the example you have chosen, consider who are like the beast that comes from the sea (that is to say, who are from outside the community), and who are the beast that comes from the earth (that is, from the neighborhood itself). You will see that, if there are exploiters from outside, that exploitation is possible because there are in the neighborhood itself those who acquiesce to that exploitation and even benefit from it. Discuss this with other people in your church and in other churches. Develop a plan of action.

Fifth Day: Read Revelation 13:16-18

See: What has most intrigued readers of this passage through the ages is the famous number of the beast, 666. There are two basic ways to interpret that number. The first is by looking for a name or phrase that adds up to 666. Since in Greek (and also in Hebrew) numbers were written with letters, if one adds the numeric values of the letters in a name, one reaches a figure. Following this method of interpretation, many possible alternatives have been suggested. One of them is the Roman Empire itself, whose name can be written in such a way that it comes to 666. Other alternatives are several emperors or rulers of the time. The most probable is that, if the number in fact originally referred to a name, it was some leader or ruler in the province of Asia whose name history has not recorded.

Also, following the same method and combining this with the view of Revelation as a program for the end times, later interpreters have suggested that the number 666 represents the Pope, Luther, Calvin, Hitler, communism, Kennedy, the European Common Market, and others.

The second method of interpretation is based on the meaning of the number 666 itself. If the number 7 represents perfection and fullness, 6 represents just the opposite. It is a number of imperfection. Then, to describe somebody or something with the number 666 is the opposite of perfection, truth, and fullness, which would be 777. In this interpretation, what the number indicates is that the beast that presents itself as powerful, invincible, and perfect, in fact is not. It is a mere 666—incomplete, imperfect, false.

At any rate, the discussion about who or what bears the number 666 has tended to eclipse the central point of the passage, which is the necessity of having the mark of the beast in order to participate in the economic life of the area. Remember what was said before about the mark of God on those who would be saved. To bear the mark of God is to belong to God. To bear the mark of the beast is to belong to the beast. Now it turns out that is that it is necessary to choose between bearing the mark of the beast and bearing the mark of God, which will result in being excluded from economic life—not being able to buy or to sell. Remember what was said while discussing the church in Thyatira, that to be able to follow an occupation it was necessary to belong to a religious guild and to serve the gods of that guild. It is to this situation that this passage refers.

Judge: Instead of spending time in useless speculation about what or who the beast is, trying to decipher the number 666, return to what you thought and wrote yesterday, on how the beast from the earth collaborates with the beast from the sea, and how this works in our own communities. Could it be true that in some cases the power of that local beast is such that if we refuse to serve it we will have to pay a very high price?

Think for instance of a neighborhood where a few absentee owners control most of the available housing. Because they have no competition, they refuse to make the necessary repairs so that people renting their properties may have a minimum of comfort and security. We may wish to do something to change that situation, but we discover that some people who belong to our church are among those who benefit as agents of the absentee owners, and that their offerings are a substantial part of the church's income. What are we to do as a church? To subsist economically we have to ignore the injustice that is taking place. If we ignore the situation, do we not we take upon ourselves the mark of the beast? And if we refuse to bear that mark, what will happen? That was the situation in which many of those Christians who first received and read Revelation found themselves.

Act: Go back to what you thought and wrote yesterday. Have you followed up by discussing this matter with other people? Are you beginning to develop a plan of action?

Sixth Day: Read Revelation 14:1-5

See: Now the counterpart of the dragon enters the picture. The Lamb appears on Mount Zion, that is to say, in Jerusalem. Although in other places of Revelation we have been told of the horns and other traits of the Lamb, here it is assumed that readers already know who the Lamb is.

Next to him there is a multitude of 144,000. As was said before, this is not an exact number, but is rather an indication of the fullness of those redeemed (12 x 12 x 1,000). In contrast to those who bear the mark of the beast, these people bear on their foreheads the name of the Lamb and of the Father.

Once again we witness the great heavenly praise, in which the multitude of the redeemed sings before the throne, before the four living creatures, and before the twenty-four elders. Nobody else, however, can learn their song; that is, whoever is not counted among this multitude and does not bear the name of the Lamb and of the Father cannot pass as one of them.

Verse 4 tells us who these people are who now sing in heaven. They are those "who have not defiled themselves with women, for they are virgins." This must not be taken literally, since the church never taught that virginity was necessary for salvation. As we have seen previously, in Revelation, as in much prophetic literature, fornication and adultery are images for idolatry. Whoever has gone after other gods has been defiled, just as if they had fornicated. Thus, this multitude consists of those people who have remained faithful even amid the tribulation. Also, they are true witnesses in whose mouths there are no lies.

Judge: The most common interpretation of Revelation reads it as a book that announces disasters and calamities. There is no doubt that this book announces great suffering for those who refuse to accept the rule of God and of the Lamb, and especially for those who persecute the faithful. But that is not the central theme of the book. The central theme is the great joy of heavenly adoration, to which all who have been redeemed by the Lamb are invited—that is to say, all those who have remained firm and who bear on their foreheads, not the sign of the beast, but the name of the Lamb and of God.

Why do you believe that, when reading Revelation, people pay so little attention to these passages that speak of heavenly worship or of the joy of heaven, and so much to the ones that speak of disasters, tribulation, and trial? Could it be that we sometimes forget that the gospel is good news, and are more interested in the sufferings and in the condemnation of unbelievers than in the grace and the love of God?

Act: If your hymnal has an index of the biblical texts that have inspired hymns, look in that index to see how many hymns have been inspired by Revelation. (The best known is possibly "Holy, holy, holy," but there are many more.) Sing or repeat the words of some of those hymns. If your hymnal does not have such an index, at least sing or repeat "Holy, holy, holy," noting that this hymn uses many of the images that we have already seen in our study of Revelation. End your period of study with a prayer asking God that, by means of your worship here on earth, you may be prepared for the joy of heavenly worship.

Seventh Day: Read Revelation 14:6-13

See: Once again, there is a series of warnings for those who refuse to obey God. In this case, the warnings come from three angels.

The first one flies "in midheaven," that is to say that it is clearly visible to all creatures, as the sun is visible at its zenith. This angel has "an eternal gospel" to proclaim everywhere and to all. Thus, no one can claim that they were not told. And the warning is clear: it is necessary to fear God and to give God the glory. In the passages that we have studied this week we have seen how the beast that comes from the earth calls all to fear and to give glory to the beast from the sea—in other words, that the local authorities, priests, and aristocracy invite all to fear Rome and to give it the glory.

In stark contrast, this angel invites all to fear and to give glory to God, "for the hour of his judgment has come." Note also that the beast whom the world worships—Rome and its might— came from the sea, and the beast that supports it has come from the earth; but the God whom all must worship made both the sea and the earth, as well as heaven and all the springs of water. The contrast is clear: whoever serves, honors, and adores the beast renders worship and honor to a false, and in the end, impotent god.

The second angel announces the fall of "Babylon." When Revelation was written, the city of Babylon no longer existed. It was a mere heap of ruins in the desert. But the name "Babylon" was still used in the Jewish literature of the time to refer to any oppressive power. This was because in earlier centuries Babylon had been the great enemy and oppressor of the Hebrews. In the eighth century before Christ, the empire that had its capital in Babylon conquered and destroyed the kingdom of the north (Israel) and its capital, Samaria, taking many of its inhabitants captive. The kingdom of the south (Judea) continued existing for some time. But in the sixth century before Christ a new Babylonian empire invaded the Kingdom of Judea, destroyed the city of Jerusalem, and took many of its inhabitants captive. Thus, for the people of Israel, the name "Babylon" was synonymous with any oppressive power; and for the same reason in the books of the prophets of the Old Testament there are frequent references to Babylon, to its wickedness, and to its fall.

The angel announces, as good news, the fall of "Babylon," which in this case is Rome and its empire. The angel further declares that the reason for this fall is that "she has made all nations drink of the wine of the wrath of her fornication." Here, as before in Revelation and many times in the prophets, "fornication" refers to idolatry, to abandoning the true God in order to go after alien and false gods. The angel's announcement resembles several texts in the Old Testament. For instance, in Isaiah 21:9 we read that "fallen, fallen is Babylon; and all the images of her gods lie shattered on the ground."

The reference to the wine that Babylon has made the nations drink is parallel to what is said in Jeremiah 51:7: "Babylon was a golden cup in the LORD's hand, making all the earth drunken; the nations drank of her wine, and so the nations went mad." Thus, although the nations drink of the cup and are intoxicated with the wine offered by Babylon/Rome, what in fact they are drinking is the wine of the wrath of God, as may be seen in Revelation 14:10.

The third angel makes the warning still clearer: all who worship the beast and its image and bear the mark of the beast will be punished. Remember that what imperial authorities required of Christians was that they worship the Emperor's image. It is to this, or to some similar requirement, that this warning refers. Whoever yields to the pressure of the authorities and worships the beast receives the mark of the beast, becomes its property, and renounces the true God. Such a person will drink of the cup of God's wrath. (Later on we will see that Revelation returns to this image of the cups of wrath.) And their punishment will be eternal ("forever and ever").

Notice in verses 11 and 13 the contrast between these people for whom "there is no rest," and the faithful who "will rest from their labors." Remember that the Sabbath or day of rest was very important in the religion of Israel. Rest is renewal. In the Bible, even God rests. Those who have ignored the divine warnings will have no rest, while those who have heeded and accepted them will enjoy an eternal Sabbath.

Judge: Once again Revelation offers warnings. Three angels announce the fall of Babylon and of the order that it represents, and at the same time proclaim the need to serve only the one true God. You will already have lost count of how many warnings have been made in this book of Revelation. If you had not studied it before, you possibly imagined that this book simply spoke of the end of the world. But much more than that, the book continues delaying the end of the world while God offers warning after warning. It is for this reason that, instead of thinking of it as a book of hate or of vengeance, we must think of Revelation as a book in which the grace of God is manifested in repeated warnings.

Remember that Jesus told his disciples that they should forgive even "seventy times seven" (Matthew 18:22 note). Since seven and ten are numbers that indicate fullness, "seventy times seven" (7 x 10 x 7) means infinity. Thus, what Jesus told his disciples to do with their enemies, God also does with God's enemies: God warns them; warns them again; and warns them again; and still warns them. Such warnings are calls to new life and offers of forgiveness. If they do not listen, it is because they simply and defiantly insist on not hearing.

God continues announcing pardon and salvation until the very last moment. Therefore, the church cannot cease in that task, even though it has preached its message more than a thousand times a thousand. The message that is good news for those who already believe must also be a warning and a loving call for those who do not believe.

Act: Several days ago you made the purpose to announce the gospel to those around you who may have already heard it, but still do not believe. Did you do it? If you did not do it, do it now. If you did, do it once again. Do it with the same love with which God has called you, without hatred nor a spirit of vengeance, but calling to newness of life those who in fact lead empty lives without God. Invite other people in your church to make a similar commitment. Meet with them to pray for those who still do not believe.

For Group Study

Ask the group to review what we have studied this week about the dragon, the beast from the sea, and the beast from the earth. Remember that the dragon is the ultimate chief of both beasts, and that the text tells us that the dragon is none other than Satan. The beast that comes from the sea represents Roman might. The beast from the earth represents the authorities and local aristocracies of the province of Asia that are ready to support and to foment Roman might.

Ask the group if they believe that the dragon/Satan is still active. Invite them to mention or suggest situations today in which they can see or suspect the activity of the dragon, perhaps through proxies such as the beast from the sea and the beast from the land. (Help them consider, for instance, whether there are social, cultural, economic, or political powers that demand that we obey them, although they may oppose the will of God, and if there are other lesser powers that impel us to obey those wider powers.)

They could also consider how such pressures are placed on their children, and what they can do to counteract them.

After the discussion, invite the group to try to discern what we can do today to resist the will of the dragon and its beasts.

W E E K
NINE

First Day: Read Revelation 14:14-16

See: The passages that we will study today and tomorrow deal once again with the theme of judgment. But now the image of a harvest is used. As we will see, there are two harvests, a good one and a bad one, one for blessing and the other for destruction. The first one, which we shall study today, is a harvest of wheat. The second one, which we shall study tomorrow, is of grapes.

Although up to this point the most frequent image to refer to Jesus Christ is the Lamb, here he is called "the Son of the Man." This phrase appears for the first time in the Bible in Daniel ("one like a son of man"—7:13–14), where it refers to the one who will exercise authority in the final judgment. It also appears in the New Testament as a way of referring to Jesus. If you read, for example, Matthew 24:30-31 or Mark 13:26-27, you will see that there it is said that the Son of Man will come in the clouds and will send angels to gather his own. Also in Matthew 25:31-46— "the judgment of the nations"—the one who judges is "the Son of Man." Naturally, in these Gospels the Son of Man is none other than Jesus Christ, who comes to seek his own. In the passage we are studying, he has a golden crown, a sign that the time for his reign has come. Along the same lines, he holds in his hand a sickle for the harvest.

An angel announces that the time has come to reap, and the Son of Man reaps the whole earth. In other words, the Son of Man is collecting his crop of good wheat.

Judge: The passages for today and tomorrow deal with the time of judgment: today's passage with the promise to the faithful, and tomorrow's with the punishment of those who are not faithful. In a sense, both are a warning. Today's text promises us that if we are faithful we shall be part of the harvest of good wheat reaped by the Son of Man.

Are we truly faithful? Do we allow ourselves to be led astray, at least in some aspects of our lives, by the attractiveness of the wrong? Are we perhaps so much a part of the society that surrounds us that many times we simply accept its values as our own? In that case, can we truly claim the promise made in this passage?

Act: Pray: Thank you, my God, because you have called me from darkness to light, from death to life. Help me so to live this life that you gave me that when the end arrives it can continue living with you, harvested by your hand as a crop of holiness. I pray in the name of Jesus Christ, the Son of Man, whose harvest I intend to be. Amen.

Second Day: Read Revelation 14:17-20

See: We come now to the other side of judgment: those who cannot inherit the kingdom. In this case, it is not the Son of Man who harvests them but an angel. What is harvested is not wheat, but grapes. These are tossed in "the great wine press of the wrath of God," and trampled in it until blood runs in enormous quantities for a long distance. (What the text says is that it flowed for a thousand six hundred stadia, which is approximately two hundred miles, as the NRSV reads.) And we are told that the blood reached "as high as a horse's bridle"—that is, about four feet—for that distance.)

The image is consistent with what we saw at the end of last week. There we saw the image of the wine of God's wrath. In today's passage those who are to be punished are compared to grapes that are trampled to press the wine out—or, since these are human beings, to press out their blood. When hearing or reading this passage, those who knew the Old Testament would remember the words of Isaiah 63:3, 6: "I have trodden the wine press alone.... I trod them in my anger and trampled them in my wrath; their juice spattered on my garments, and stained all my robes."

Judge: Today's passage is one more of the many warnings that appear in Revelation against sinful people and unbelievers. Up to this point, every time we have seen one of those warnings we may have taken for granted that God is warning others, those who do not belong to the church. But it is important that we stop to consider the possibility that those warnings may also be for us. We call ourselves believers, and we really are. But are we faithful? Do we allow ourselves to be led away by the attractiveness of evil—or, as Revelation would say, by the glory of the beast?

After calling others to repentance, it is good if we apply to ourselves the same measure, that we therefore take these warnings as directed to us, and that we repent.

During the Civil War in the United States, some made use of this imagery in Revelation to interpret what was taking place then. That is why the "Battle Hymn of the Republic" says, "He is trampling out the vintage where the grapes of wrath are stored." Do you see any situations today where similar applications of this passage could be made?

Act: Pray: Forgive me, my God, that in spite of having known and accepted your gospel I have not always been faithful. I have sometimes left you in order to go after other things of less value but apparently more attractive. *[Mention some of them here.]* Forgive me, for the love of your Son Jesus Christ, the Lamb, that was slaughtered by me. And give me the faith, the patience, and the strength to be faithful. By Jesus Christ, the faithful witness, your Son and my Lord. Amen.

Third Day: Read Revelation 15: 1-4

See: The passage begins by declaring that John saw a sign in heaven. This phrase is only used two other times in Revelation:

when the woman clothed with the sun appears, and when the great dragon appears (12:1, 3). What John now sees is seven angels, each one with a plague. And he adds that these are the last plagues, for with them the wrath of God is completed.

But, as in so many other occasions in this book, instead of proceeding immediately to describe each of the seven plagues, John turns to the celestial worship once again. In that worship, those who have attained victory (remember how frequently victory and conquering are mentioned in the seven letters) stand beside the sea of glass, which is also mentioned in 4:6.

These people sing "the song of Moses" and "the song of the Lamb." The reference to Moses would remind readers of Moses' praise upon leaving Egypt and, in consequence, also of the plagues that were necessary to achieve that victory. Once again, the seven final plagues repeatedly remind us of the plagues in Egypt. The hymn is a song of praise for what God has done and it includes the promise that "all nations will come and worship before you."

Judge: Remember what was said much earlier about Revelation as a drama that unfolds on two stages—one on earth and the other in heaven. Here we are once again in heaven, where the angels get ready to pour out their cups of wrath, and where the choir of the redeemed sings to God. Christians have repeatedly been charged with thinking of heaven and therefore forgetting the earth. But it is not so with John. On the contrary, John speaks of what happens on earth, and sometimes he even refers quite directly to the economic and political problems of the time. But he does this always having in mind an added perspective—a perspective derived from his vision of what takes place in heaven.

Today many believers are convinced that the Christian life is not only a matter of looking up to heaven and rejoicing in the promise of life eternal, but that the Christian life should be lived here on earth with full knowledge of our responsibilities. They are correct, but unfortunately, if this idea is taken to the extreme, then we imagine that there are no more realities than those we see and that only earthly social, political, moral, and economic events are important. The truth is that as believers we should try to develop a perspective similar to that of John on Patmos: to see what happens on earth with realistic eyes, but to see it in the light of what we know happens in heaven. We have to learn how to connect the facts of daily life with a perspective of eternity. We have to remember that, even when things seem otherwise, in the end the last word belongs to God and to the Lamb. Without that there is no true Christian obedience. It is for that reason that, even when speaking of what happens on the earth, John repeatedly relates it to his vision of heavenly worship.

Act: Take this morning's newspaper. Read the headlines on the first page. Try to imagine what John would say about each one of them. Where and how is God acting in today's history? Where do we see signs of the beast? From now on, every time you read the newspaper or listen to the news, try placing everything in the light of what, as a believer, you know: that the victory belongs to the Lamb. Discuss this with other people in church. If possible, meet from time to time to discuss the events of the day or of the week, always from the perspective of what we know of God's plans and promises.

Fourth Day: Read Revelation 15:5-8

See: John returns to the seven angels with seven plagues that he introduced at the beginning of the chapter. But now their entrance is more dramatic, and their appearance is described in more detail. The celestial temple opens up—in itself already a prodigious event—and from it emerge the seven angels dressed in clothes that indicate authority. It is one of the four living creatures that gives them the seven cups, full of the wrath of God.

The text does not explain the relationship between the earlier plagues and these seven cups of wrath. In fact, as the action unfolds later on, at times they seem to be the same. Once again, we should remember that the language of the book of Revelation is poetic and allusive, rather that prosaic and descriptive. The central point of the passage is that these angels bring the fullness of the destructive power of the wrath of God that will be manifested in plagues upon the earth. With these plagues the wrath of God will be completely played out.

Then the temple is filled with smoke, which is a sign of the power and the glory of God (see Exodus 19:18 and Isaiah 4:5), and from that point on nobody can enter the temple. What this means is that we have come to the moment of the final trial. Up to now we have seen a series of warnings. But the end belongs only to God. It is already much too late to want to come closer to the presence of God. What is more, when everything has been fulfilled the temple itself will disappear (see Revelation 21:22).

Judge: In general, in church we do not hear much about the wrath of God. Sometimes we even seem to think that anger is not compatible with a God of love. But it is not so. The sanctity of God cannot tolerate the permanent existence of evil. In the end, evil must be destroyed. Certainly, God forgives. Were it not so, there would be no hope for any of us. But forgiveness by itself does not suffice to destroy evil.

The wrath of God is not an irrational rage or a vindictive spite. It is rather an aspect of God's very love that wishes creatures to live in holiness. Thus the divine anger is part of redemption. It is part of the saving plan of God. What is more, when reading the whole book of Revelation, we see that the anger of God is directed primarily against the sources of evil—that is to say, against the dragon and the beast. But if there are humans who insist on serving the beast, they too will have to suffer the wrath of God.

Act: Pray: Lord, we know that you are a holy God and that you cannot tolerate evil before your presence. Clean and sanctify us, so we may be in your presence and sing your praise with the heavenly choir. Do not allow us to forget your wrath that requires sanctity, or your love that promises pardon. By Jesus Christ, the slaughtered Lamb who is to be the life of all. Amen.

Fifth Day: Read Revelation 16:1-7

See: The seven angels seem to have been waiting for the order to pour out their bowls of wrath. Although they are the ones who hold these cups, it is God who determines the times and directs the action.

The plagues that these angels will pour on the earth remind us of the ten plagues God unleashed against the Egyptians so they would grant freedom to the people of Israel. They also remind us of the plagues that God warns Moses will come to the people if they are not faithful and if they themselves become oppressors (Leviticus 26:1-3).

The first three angels pour their cups one after another, in rapid succession. The first produces "a foul and painful sore" on those who have the mark of the beast. In a way, what this does is to mark more prominently and exactly those who serve the beast. One can hide human loyalties with relative ease. When seeing people, it is not possible to know immediately who serves the beast and who serves God. But this plague points out who the servants of the beast are. The very foulness of the sores lays bare the corruption that lurks behind all service to the beast.

The second cup of wrath turns the sea into blood. This is similar to one of the plagues of Egypt, except that now it is the whole sea that becomes bloody, and it is a blood that smells of death and produces the death of all that lives in the sea. (Remember that in the previous warnings what was destroyed was a fourth or a third of what existed. Since these are no longer warnings, but a final judgment, the wrath reaches the whole.)

The third cup brings similar consequences, but now they affect the fresh waters. It is then that "the angel of the waters" intones a hymn that affirms the justice of God that now forces those who spilled the blood of the saints to drink blood. To this hymn another voice responds from the altar, like an antiphon that also affirms the justice of God.

Judge: Remember that the plagues of the Old Testament include those of Egypt as well as the ones that God promises to the people of Israel if they in turn become oppressors. The church and its members have to remember this, because when reading of these plagues we assume too easily that they are plagues that reach only those who do not believe. But God warned Israel that, if the people who had been liberated from slavery became oppressors, plagues would fall on them similar to those that fell on Egypt.

If the church and its members—we who have been liberated from the yoke of sin by the blood of the Lamb—forget the grace of God and become oppressors, or if in any other way we allow ourselves to be led by the beast, the wrath of God will come on us also. Thus, when reading this passage we should take care not to say to ourselves, "Thankfully our enemies will be destroyed!" If they are our enemies because we have oppressed them, or because we have not given good witness before them, then the wrath of God will also come on us.

On the other hand, notice that what the first plague does is to show what was already there: the mark of the beast becomes a visible and foul sore. Part of God's judgment is precisely laying evil bare, so that it can then be destroyed.

Act: Pray: I thank you, God of the ages and of the nations, that your justice will overcome. I thank you that you have washed me in the blood of the Lamb. I ask that right now, while there is still time, you show me the evil that may still dwell in me and that you sanctify me so that I can be in your presence. By Jesus Christ, the Sacred Lamb. Amen.

Sixth Day: Read Revelation 16:8-14

See: After the interlude of the two hymns (one from the angel of the water and the other from the altar), follow the fourth, fifth, and sixth plagues.

The fourth angel pours his cup not on the earth but on the sun, whose heat multiplies to the point of burning people on earth. But even while they burn, they continue blaspheming against God and do not repent.

The fifth angel pours his cup on the very throne of the beast, and what follows is a great darkness (which also reminds us of one of the plagues of Egypt). Notice that in a way this plague is just the opposite of the previous one. In one the sun burned too bright. In the other, the result is darkness. But neither plague makes people repent, nor do they cease their blasphemies.

When the sixth angel pours his cup, the river Euphrates dries up. This river had been the traditional border between the Roman Empire and Persia. Now that it has dried, the road is open for an invasion from the east. But this does not mean that everything will be completed in a mere battle between the kings of the east and Rome. Instead, we are told that from the mouths of the powers of evil foul spirits like frogs emerge (which also reminds us of another of the plagues of Egypt). Those spirits go and convince the kings of the whole earth to join them in the battle against God.

What happens here is interesting. At other moments in biblical history, God had used pagan kings (for instance, Cyrus) to carry forth God's will. Those who first heard the reading of this book would expect that, in drying up the river Euphrates, God would now use the Persians to invade and destroy Rome. But no. In this final battle that is brewing, all the kings of the earth take the side of the dragon.

Judge: What does all this mean? It means that we are coming to the moment of judgment, when there is no longer time for repentance or regrets. Those who did not listen to the previous warnings will not listen to the last ones.

In a way, this is a final warning for us. We sometimes think that, since we are believers, we have already come closer to the kingdom, and when the moment arrives we will repent for whatever sins we still practice. For the time being, there is no need to worry too much. But here we are told otherwise: if we do not heed the present warnings, the moment will come when it will be much too late for repentance.

The other interesting element in this passage is that now all the kings of the earth get ready to war against God. On other occasions, God could use some kings against others. But now, when the moment of the final battle approaches, the final loyalty of those kings is manifested. The powerful want to conserve their power; and at the moment of ultimate decision, when what is at stake is the coming of a new kingdom, all the kings are in agreement against such a new order.

This should also serve as warning that one of the privileges of the present order that is most difficult to surrender is power. The powerful seek to conserve their power at all costs. That is another form in which they serve the dragon, and will be shown as such. What are we to say, then, of the way in which some of us cling to power—even though it may be only the minimal power that we have in the church? What are we to say of those power struggles that appear so frequently in our meetings and our committees? It is sad and harsh to say so, but that too is service to the dragon.

Act: Examine your own life and your relationships. In some of those relationships, it is very probable that you have power over other people (although these may be only your children or an employee). That is not necessarily bad. Without structures of authority neither the world nor the church could function. But if you cling to power, or if you end up loving that power for its own sake, or if you use it to oppress or to exploit other people, you are serving the beast. Ultimately, you are like those kings of the earth who took the side of the dragon against God when the moment of the final decision was at hand.

Make a careful analysis of your relationships of power and how you use whatever power you have. Place it all before God and pray that God will teach you to use power properly, or if not, will take it away from you.

Seventh Day: Read Revelation 16:15-21

See: At this time the narrative is interrupted with words from the Lord. They are similar to others that we find in the Gospels (for instance, Matthew 24:43-44), in the epistles (1 Thessalonians

5:2), and even in Revelation itself (3:18). They constitute a warning and a reminder for the faithful who must wait for the Lord without knowing when he will come. Once again, the purpose of Revelation is not to serve us as program that tells us exactly when and how the end will come, but rather to exhort us to live in such a way that we are always ready for the day of the Lord. This warning is so important that the culminating point of the narrative is interrupted to remind us of it.

Then follows the famous reference to *Harmagedon*. So much has been said about that subject that it possibly surprises us to know that this is the only passage in the whole Bible in which the word *Harmagedon* appears. No place in ancient geography is known by that name, although some think it is a variant of "Megiddo," a place where some important battles in the Old Testament took place (Judges 5:19; 1 Kings 22:29; 2 Chronicles 35:22). It is surprising how many theories and doctrines on the final battle have been developed on the basis of this word whose exact meaning is not known.

When the seventh angel pours his bowl, he pours it into the air. We are not told directly what the results of this cup are. But a dramatic event follows its being poured out: a voice from the temple in heaven declares, "It is done!" It is probably the voice of God who finally declares the divine plan fulfilled. The God who at the beginning said, "Let there be," and all that God pronounced was made—that same God now declares, "It is done!" And the voice of God resounds in lightning, rumblings, and thunder, and the worst earthquake ever.

Then the last plague is finally described. It combines that great earthquake with enormous hail. The earthquake is such that the islands and the mountains disappear. And the hail is such that each grain weighs a talent (some hundred pounds). The "great city" (probably Rome) is broken in three, and the other cities are equally destroyed. Babylon, until then so powerful and proud, has to present itself before God to drink of the chalice of divine wrath. But in spite of all this, and even as a response to it, people curse the name of God rather than repent. As we have seen in the case of the previous plagues, in this final series it is already much too late for repentance. All that is left is to drink of the wrath of God.

Judge: That the cups of wrath do not lead people to repent should not surprise us. If all the previous warnings were not enough to convert these people, these new plagues will not achieve a different result. Those who chose to follow the beast did so because it seemed to be almighty. But once they have committed their life to the beast, it is very difficult to abandon it. As the struggle intensifies, they are drawn to an even deeper commitment to the beast. This commitment reaches such a point that when it becomes clear that the beast will not have the last word, all these people can do is curse God—in other words, reaffirm their service to the beast.

For those who have committed to the service of the beast, each new warning, each new plague, each new difficulty, is a threat to their lifestyle, to their security. It is for that reason that it is so difficult to move away from that path once it is taken. For that reason, John warns his readers with such insistence about the insidious power of the beast.

All this seems very theoretical. Or it seems to apply only in extreme circumstances, like those confronting the church when John wrote, when the Roman Empire demanded that it be rendered a glory and worship that only God deserves. But is our situation in fact so different from what it was then? Certainly, at least in most of the countries of the world, Christians are no longer persecuted for their faith. Today nobody tells us that if we do not adore the emperor we will be fed to the beast in the circus. But precisely for that reason the power of the beast may be even more insidious, introducing itself into our lives without our even noticing it. Let us see some cases.

Some days ago I mentioned the case of my friend whose company put him to work designing guidance systems for nuclear weapons. As I said then, my friend surrendered his employment rather than devote his life to building weapons that could kill thousands and millions of innocent victims. But in a similar corporation there was another engineer who had begun to work there some years earlier than my friend. He was an active member of a denomination that has been characterized by its commitment to peace and its rejection of violence and war. When this particular company offered him employment, some people in his church warned him that it would be difficult to work there without having to commit to violence. He explained that his work was in another section, designing television sets. He began to work there, married a woman from the church, and they bought a beautiful house. Time passed, and one day he was offered a promotion in the company and a significant salary increase. He would be made supervisor of an entire division that worked with radars. Some of their products would be components for the division that built nuclear weapons.

His wife was not very happy with those new responsibilities. But it meant a salary increase that would help with the education of their children and the mortgage on the house. Little by little, this man became more and more involved in the production of nuclear weapons, and eventually he came to direct most of that entire project. People in his church told him it seemed that he was no longer as involved as he used to be and that he no longer attended with the same regularity. His wife told him that she was concerned because his disposition was changing. Things continued along the same path. While he earned more and more money, he continued moving away from his community of faith and eventually from his Christian commitment. The last I heard about him was that he had physically abused his wife and that she had fled with their children, leaving him alone in their enormous empty house, still insisting that he was happy with his good position in the company.

It is not necessary to go that far to see that, when the beast is surreptitiously introduced into our lives and stakes a claim on them, it is sometimes very difficult to free ourselves from its power, no matter how many warnings and even plagues may assail us.

Act: Examine your commitments in life. Begin with your social commitments. Think, for instance, of people with whom you relate. How do you relate to them? Can you do it conserving your Christian integrity, or do these relationships tempt you to compromise that integrity? For example, there are "friends" who we know do us no good and in whose company we do not dare speak of our faith. If they do us no good, are we doing such people any good? If not, why do we conserve such friendships?

Now move on to your economic commitments. Examine the way in which you earn and spend your money. Are they compatible with your faith? Or are you compromising that faith for a few dollars or for a little more comfort?

Repeat this process with all the other commitments you have in life.

Write down your reflections. Pray over them.

For Group Study

Discuss with the group the following questions:

Is it true that the time comes when people are so committed to evil that they do not abandon it, no matter how many warnings they have of the consequences of their chosen paths?

Is it true that the power of evil (the beast) is sometimes introduced silently into the life of people, so that by the time we discover what is happening the damage is already such that it is very difficult for us to change our ways?

In the discussion on each one of these questions make sure that the group keeps in mind what we have studied of Revelation, and that they use examples taken from real and daily life.

W E E K
TEN

First Day: Read Revelation 17:1-5

See: We come now to one of the most famous passages in the whole book. Notice that John does not claim that all these visions follow a particular order or that they refer to the final events of history. Here, it is one of the angels with the seven cups of wrath who shows him the vision; and it is clear that those cups of wrath have not yet been poured on the earth, since the great harlot is infatuated with her power and there are no signs that this power has been destroyed or even threatened. Once again, we must read Revelation as what it is: a series of visions with powerful dreamlike imagery.

Those who first heard the reading of these lines, in churches such as those in Ephesus and Sardis, would know that John was referring to Rome. Rome is the one seated on the great scarlet beast. It is the capital of the Empire, determining its direction just as a rider determines the direction of a steed. With Rome the kings of the earth have fornicated. Remember what was said about fornication as an image for idolatry; this means that the kings have joined her in her idolatry. Once again, remember that the Roman Empire included many kingdoms whose kings were Rome's subjects and agents. All those kings and peoples have been intoxicated with the wine of Rome—they have drunk of the power of Rome that leads to oppression and idolatry.

The woman is dressed in purple and scarlet. The first color is a sign of imperial power, and the second of death and destruction. (Purple dye being extremely expensive, purple clothing was worn only by the very rich and powerful, normally emperors and their high representatives. Scarlet was the color of blood, so its connection with death and violence is obvious.) The chalice in her hand, golden but full of abominations and impurities, is a symbol of the power and prestige of Rome: shiny, yet also foul.

The name on her forehead indicates who the woman is and how Christians must interpret her power: "Babylon the great, mother of whores and of earth's abominations."

Judge: The words that John sent to the churches of Asia were a strong condemnation of the Roman Empire and its policies. When today we speak in church, do we dare point out the evils of our day and their origins with equal clarity? Or do we speak simply of "sin," never saying who promotes evil and benefits from it? What do you think would happen if in your church people followed John's lead in discussing the evils of our day?

Act: Think of some specific evil in your neighborhood or community. If possible, choose an evil of which other people are conscious. (It can be the sale of drugs, unemployment, abusive rents, the exploitation of women, or anything else.) Analyze the situation by asking two questions: (1) What are the roots of that evil—that is, who benefits from it and who promotes it? (2) Are those roots ever named in your church? Should they be named? Write down your reflections and share them with leaders in your church.

Second Day: Read Revelation 17:6

See: We were told earlier that the woman had in her hand a golden chalice full of abominations. Now we are also told that she is drunk with the foulness of her chalice. That foulness is the blood of the saints and the blood of Jesus' witnesses. In other words, the woman is cheerful and celebrating because she has persecuted and destroyed those who were faithful to God.

John's amazement can also be interpreted as perplexity. John does not know how to interpret what he sees, an image of the power of evil. Could it be that evil is so powerful that it will triumph? What will become of the church, persecuted by such a rich and powerful harlot?

Judge: Return to what you thought and wrote yesterday. The powers of evil that you mentioned then are certainly powerful. They are so powerful that they cause astonishment. If you imagine that they could be defeated easily, you probably have not taken account of all their power. Think of those powers as dressed in purple—a sign of their authority—and adorned with gold, precious stones, and pearls—signs of wealth—and then you will begin to see how powerful are the enemies that Christians must oppose.

Act: Make an inventory of the resources and allies on which the powers of evil you considered yesterday can count. Continue making that inventory until fear and perplexity overwhelm you. Only then will you be able to understand the difficult struggle before the church as it seeks to be faithful.

Remember that what Revelation promises is the fall of Babylon—and of all the modern Babylons that become drunk with the blood of the faithful, oppress the weak, and promote vice and wickedness.

Close your study session with a prayer asking God to show you how great is the power of today's Babylons, but also to show you how much greater is God's power.

Third Day: Read Revelation 17:7-9

See: Here the angel begins explaining to John who this woman is whom he sees. In verse 9 there is one of the clearest indications that the harlot is Rome. Indeed, it was customary to speak of Rome as the city built on seven hills. Thus, to say that the seven heads of the beast represent seven mountains on which the harlot sits is a fairly clear way of saying that the harlot is none other than the city of Rome.

The most difficult phrase in this passage is the cryptic declaration, which appears twice with slight variations in verse 8, that the beast "was and is not and is to come." There have been many different interpretations of this phrase, and none of them is certain. Most probably it is setting up a contrast and a parallelism between the beast and the Lord "who is and who was and who is to come" (Revelation 1:4, 8; 4:8). As in so many other things, the beast is a parody of the Lamb. But notice that the beast comes from the abyss, while the Lord comes from heaven.

Judge: Repeatedly in Revelation the beast is presented as an imitation or parody of the Lamb. It is important to emphasize this, because we sometimes think that the difference between good and evil is so clear that the one cannot pass for the other. But it is not so. The most dangerous idols are those which most resemble the true God. The worst enemies of Christ are those who look like him and hide their wickedness under a mantle of religiosity. Could it be that our worst temptations are those that present themselves in imitation of true faith and obedience?

Many dictators have seized power by claiming to be saviors of their homeland and redeemers of the oppressed. Likewise, a false form of Christianity has spread all over the world—a false Christianity that claims that all God requires of us is that we attend worship and make offerings to the church. In fact what God requires of us is much more than that: that we obey God in everything—in religion, in morals, in politics, in the economy, and in our family relationships.

Act: Consider if there are in your life false gods—things, desires, dreams, goals, relationships—that masquerade as fidelity and obedience when they are in fact temptations to disobedience. Name them. Toss them out. Ask the true God for help in distinguishing God's will from all that the false gods of this world tell us to do.

Fourth Day: Read Revelation 17:10-14

See: The explanation of the vision continues. As in any vision, the images have more than a single meaning and they sometimes meld into one another. Thus, the seven heads that in verse 9 were seven mountains now in verse 10 are seven kings. And the beast, besides having those seven heads that are kings, is itself a king, the eighth, and still also one of the seven. And later we are told that there are ten other kings that are the ten horns, and that they do not reign yet.

What we have here is probably a double metaphor. On one hand, the numbers seven and ten are used in their usual sense of fullness. But there is also a reference to certain legends regarding Nero. Let us consider these two metaphors in order.

In the first place, there are seven kings, of which five have passed from the scene. This means that the faithful ones live amid the times whose fullness has not been completed. There have been kings and governments in the past, and kings and governments there will be in the future, until the end of history. What is more, in the future there will still be ten more kings—an entire fullness of kings and governments—who have not even ascended to their thrones. But one thing is certain: those kings will also serve the beast. In summary, Revelation has little trust in the power of governments to resist the power of evil, and it warns its readers that even if the present kingdom seems to be the height of wickedness the end is not yet.

Second, the passage refers to the legend, fairly well known at the time, that Nero, who was considered evil incarnate, would return from among the dead to terrify the world. It is probably to this that verse 11 refers when saying that among the seven kings there is one that was already, who is also the beast itself, and who will be the eighth of the kings.

In any event, the main point in the passage is not in these somewhat obscure verses, but rather in one that is quite clear: verse 14, where it is affirmed that the final victory will belong to the Lamb and to the faithful.

Judge: Why do you believe there are so many people who read Revelation to try to figure out all the mysteries of the last times and to discover when the Lord will come? Could it be that in fact this is a way of avoiding the call to obedience?

Consider the following: The only advantage we would have if we knew the exact moment of the coming of the Lord would be that we could get ready for it at the appropriate time and not before. In other words, we could continue in our evil ways until the final moment was approaching. If, on the other hand, we do not know when that moment will be, we have to be constantly obedient, for the Lord comes, as he himself says, unexpectedly, "like a thief in the night." Thus, the urge to know "the times and the seasons" is either mere useless curiosity, or the desire not to have to be constantly vigilant in obedience and service to the Lord.

Act: Pray: Forgive me, Lord, for the many times when I have wanted to read your Word out of curiosity, and not as a means to be more obedient. And forgive me also for the many times when I have been disobedient, trusting that you would not come just then. Teach me to live every day as if you were coming that evening, and every night as if you were coming at sunrise. Amen.

Fifth Day: Read Revelation 17:15-18

See: Once again it is clear that the harlot is the city of Rome. To verify it, one only needs to read verse 18 again: "The woman that you saw is the great city that rules over the kings of the earth."

According to the angel's explanation, the waters where the harlot sits are a multitude of peoples and nations. To understand this, it is necessary to remember that most trade at that time took place over rivers and seas. Land transport was expensive and slow. For that reason, one way to say that a city was rich was to describe it as seated on many waters—that is to say, receiving the benefits of far-reaching trade. Thus, what is meant here is that the wealth of Rome does not belong only to her, but rather that she has extracted it, as is the case of all empires, from other countries, nations, and peoples.

Notice also that the ten kings, although allies of the beast, will become enemies of the harlot. John has an understanding of the way of international conflicts. These kings will destroy the harlot. But for that reason they do not cease being allies of the beast. In other words, the harlot (Rome and her empire) is but an expression of the power of the beast. Other expressions of that power will arise (the ten kings), so that even while helping to destroy the harlot these kings will continue serving the beast.But this does not mean that God does not have the last word. On the contrary, what the ten kings do is also a service to God, even though they themselves do not know it.

Judge: In the concrete life of each generation, the beast uses different instruments. If we remain at the level of politics and of nations, to which this vision refers most directly, we have to say that the twentieth century saw the rise and fall of several "kings" or governments through which the beast acted. Each one of them was finally destroyed by other nations, governments, or "kings." When that happened, some Christians may have been under the illusion that, because the new "king" or nation or empire destroyed another that served the beast, this new order must be necessarily good. What has actually happened is that many have become disillusioned, seeing that the new powers also serve the beast.

In the face of such situations, Revelation teaches us several things:

First, that as believers we have to recognize and to denounce the power of the beast wherever it appears.

Second, that when other powers arise, we can see in that the action of God, rejoice in it, and even participate in the emergence of a new order or government.

Third, that we must always be alert, because the new order can well become another instrument of the beast, and in that case we have to recognize and denounce that fact just as we did with the predecessor.

Fourth, and most important, that in the end power belongs to God and to the Lamb, and that for this reason we can fight and stand firm, trusting that the victory does not depend on us.

Act: Think of the political situation in which you live. Consider if in some way John would say that you live under the power of the beast, and why—in other words, where and how does injustice appear in your society or community. Discuss this with other people in your church. Try to discover what powers oppose the evils you see. Look for ways of destroying the injustice that you or others experience. But at the same time, remember that the new powers and institutions that arise can also be placed in the service of evil, and that therefore your commitment to them must not be absolute. Only God deserves an absolute commitment.

Sixth Day: Read Revelation 18:1-3

See: Once again the fall of Babylon (Rome) is announced. Since we saw the same thing earlier (Revelation 14:8), we may assume that this is a parallel vision to that other one. Remember that Revelation should be read not as a program for the end of the world, but as a series of visions on how the power of God and the power of the dragon act. Some of those visions refer to the same thing as others. In this case particular case, we have a new announcement of the fall of Babylon/Rome.

Although the message is of destruction, there is a certain tone of joy in the angel's announcement. The fall of Babylon is due to its many fornications (idolatries) with the kings of the earth.

Once again, as in other passages that we have studied, Revelation shows that it is a matter not only of the political and military power of Rome, but also of the economic and social order that supports that power. It is for that reason that the text declares, "The merchants of the earth have grown rich from the power of her luxury." In other words, not only have the kings submitted to her power, but also the entire economic order has been diverted to serve the beast.

Judge: The Roman Empire was one of the largest and most stable of all antiquity. It was just over three hundred years after John's vision that Rome fell before the invasions of the Goths.

When that happened there was great lament, because it seemed that the world had come to an end, or at least that civilization would disappear.

That is a very normal reaction when there is any political change of importance. Faced with the fall of governments or of political parties, we fear what will follow, and for that reason we mourn what existed before. As the Spanish saying goes, "Better a known evil than an unknown good." But the reaction of Revelation to such change is very different. Rome fell for its sins. Every empire falls and will fall for its sins. Sometimes that happens when least expected. (Remember what happened in the blink of an eye to the Soviet empire.) Before those apparent political catastrophes, Revelation invites us to remember that history is in the hands of God, and that every government or empire that serves the beast will eventually fall.

Act: Pray: Teach me, Lord God, to look at the political vicissitudes of my days as John saw those of his time, so that through them I may see your hand, judgment, and power. Remind me at each step that in the end the kingdoms of the earth belong to the Lamb that was slaughtered, and that therefore all kingdoms, nations, and earthly governments deserve only limited service. I pray in the name of Jesus Christ, the slaughtered Lamb and the sovereign of the rulers of the earth. Amen.

Seventh Day: Read Revelation 18:4-24

See: The passage we study today is quite long. It deals again with the fall of Rome, and the reactions of different sorts of people. Verses 21-24 describe that fall by saying that it will be as sudden as a millstone that sinks in the sea. In fact, that is the way that most of the great empires of history have fallen. When it was thought that they were strong and invincible, at that very moment their weakness has been shown and in a short time they have succumbed.

Among the various reactions that are described in this passage is the response of "the kings of the earth" (verses 9-10).

These powerful people who for a while supported the great city now look from afar, as if they did not wish to have anything to do with it, and they mourn its destruction.

Verses 11-17*a* describe the reaction of "the merchants of the earth." Repeatedly we have seen in Revelation an awareness of how merchants and other people grow rich through their participation in the policies of the Roman Empire, and how this works to the detriment of many other people. (Remember, for example, what we saw when studying Revelation 6:5-6 and 17:15.) In this passage, therefore, there is an extensive lament on the part of the merchants, and a long list of the goods with which they have become rich. Notice that they are mostly luxury items. Notice also the reference to the traffic of slaves—"human . . . souls" (verse 13). In any event, it is clear that the merchants complain because they have lost their most important market.

In verses 17*b*-19 it is the sailors who complain, because they also have lived with the help of the trade of the great city, and now they see it disappear.

In contrast with all this, in verses 4-6 and 20 there is an indication of how believers will react. Before the fall of Rome and of their empire, they are told: "Come out of her, . . . so that you do not take part in her sins," and after its fall they are told to rejoice because God's justice has prevailed. Naturally, the believers to whom John addresses these lines could not leave the Roman Empire in the sense of going to live elsewhere. Thus, the passage exhorts them to move away from the abominations of the order in which they live and not to take part in them, although the price is high. (Remember what we said when studying the letter to Thyatira: those who refused to participate in the worship of the gods of their guilds would find it difficult to make a living. For such people, to leave Rome would mean to stay away from such worship.)

Judge: How can we today leave the modern Babylon? Think first of all the various forms Babylon takes. What follows is only one of these forms, but you can think of others.

Most of us have in our house a television set. Through it we learn many good things. But through it we are also presented repeatedly with some messages that are a present incarnation of the apocalyptic beast. We are told, for instance, that in order to be somebody it is necessary to buy, to possess, to outshine. In a way, that is the purpose of commercial television: to convince us to spend money for those things that the merchants of the earth want to sell, although we may have no need of them. Also, and almost as in passing, television tells us repeatedly that the best solution for many problems is violence. And we are also told that a disordered and even promiscuous sexual life is normal and healthy.

Before such a thing, to leave Babylon means to resist such messages. It means to view television with a critical eye—critical from a Christian perspective. It means to refuse to buy certain things, precisely because there is an attempt to force us to buy them. It means not to watch certain programs, even though we might enjoy them.

Act: When today you turn on your television set, look at it with a critical eye. Do not let yourself be carried away by its messages. During commercials, turn down the volume and discuss with your family what you have seen. Is it worthy of imitation? Write down the results of your conversation. Share it with other people who are following this study of Revelation.

For Group Study

As preparation for the group study, record about five or six minutes of television commercials. After studying the passage and what is said above, show the tape to the group and guide them in a discussion about the commercials they have seen. What do they tell us? What do they invite us to do? What values do they promote?

W E E K

ELEVEN

First Day: Read Revelation 19:1-5

See: The events that were described in the passages that we studied last week have caused great consternation among the kings and merchants of the earth, and even among sailors. But Christians must see them otherwise, as a manifestation of God's power and justice.

Now we are told that the response in heaven to those events is a great act of celestial praise. In heaven, "a great multitude" praises God precisely because God's justice has resulted in the downfall of Babylon/Rome, so that "the smoke goes up from her for ever and ever"—in other words, the memory of her destruction will remain.

Judge: As our study has progressed, you will have begun to see why Revelation is written in that mysterious and symbolic form that has intrigued some people and upset others. It is a book written in the Roman Empire, by a person exiled by the imperial authorities who, however, announces the fall of the Empire and says that when that happens there will be joy in heaven. And, as if that were not enough, the book exhorts its readers not to cooperate with the goals of the Empire, as we saw yesterday. Such a book, were it to fall by mistake into the hands of the imperial authorities, could cause a much worse persecution than already existed. Its author would be accused of subversion and sentenced to death. And the same would happen to the addressees of the book. For that reason, much of what is said is expressed in terms that only believers could understand, so that if the book were read by outsiders, it would appear to them to be no more than a series of meaningless ravings.

In any event, what John says here is that when the fall of Babylon/Rome takes place, there will be great rejoicing in heaven. His purpose throughout the book is to invite believers to look at events that take place on earth not with earthly eyes, but rather from the perspective of heaven. With earthly eyes the kings, merchants, and sailors see a great tragedy. But from the point of view of heaven, what has happened is an act of justice and a great victory for God and for God's people.

Act: Pray: Help me, Lord, to see what happens in my life and around me not with purely earthly eyes but with the vision of those who worship and praise you with the heavenly multitudes, so that I may praise you for your great works and your great salvation.

Second Day: Read Revelation 19:6-10

See: The heavenly liturgy continues, now praising God not only for the great victory but also because the time for the marriage of the Lamb has arrived. Its spouse is the church—that is to say, all the faithful. Remember that the theme of the church as the bride of Christ appears elsewhere in Scripture (for instance, Ephesians 5:23), just as in the Hebrew Scriptures the people of Israel are often depicted as the bride of God. In today's passage she is described as dressed in fine linen. Notice the contrast between this and the attire and adornments of the great harlot. The bride of Christ is dressed in good and clean clothes, but without extravagant luxuries such as those of the great harlot. And this "fine linen" that clothes the bride is "the righteous deeds of the saints." In other words, the only decoration that the church wears is the actions of its members.

The angel orders John to write a word of promise. The fact that he is expressly ordered to write indicates that this is the main point of the whole vision: the blessedness of those who are invited to the feast of the Lamb—that is, of those who have been the faithful. (Notice also that, as in so many other parts of this book, the metaphor changes in the middle of the passage. At one point, the faithful ones are the members of the bride. At another they are the guests in the wedding feast.)

In any event, the wedding feast of the Lamb, besides being a great celebration, is the declaration that from that point on, the Lamb and its bride (us) will always be together and nothing will separate them.

Last, at the end of the passage, John is ready to adore the angel, who forbids it, declaring that only God is worthy of adoration.

Judge: Think of the contrast between the great harlot and the bride of the Lamb. One is dressed in splendid raiment and covered with precious stones, but commits adultery with the kings of the earth. The other is dressed more simply, but with good taste, and her only adornment is the righteous and just works of the faithful. Could it be that sometimes, when the church wants to have power, to show that it is important, to build more and more expensive buildings, to rub shoulders with the powerful, it resembles more the great harlot than the bride of Christ?

Notice also how easy it is to slip into idolatry. Even John himself, the seer and messenger of God, after all his visions, is willing to worship a creature—an angel, true, but still a creature and not the Creator.

Act: Apply all this to the ministry of your church or community of faith. Remember that what makes it beautiful is not its many jewels—buildings, prestige, money, organization, theologians, and so on—but the righteous lives of its members. Determine that, at least today, you will adorn the church with a work of righteousness.

Third Day: Read Revelation 19:11-16

See: Once again, John has a vision of Jesus Christ. And once again, this is not a sweet and languid Jesus, but one who is powerful, victorious, and just. He comes mounted on a white horse, similar to the one that appears in Revelation 6:2. But while that other rider had the crown of power "given to him," Jesus has power from himself. He is called "Faithful and True," and "he judges and makes war" "in righteousness"—or in justice, for in Greek the two words are the same. Reaffirming some of his earlier descriptions of Jesus, John tells us that "his eyes are like a flame of fire," that he has a secret name, and that out of his mouth comes a sharp sword. To this, other elements are added along similar lines, some reminding us of what was said about the son of the woman clothed in the sun or of the various plagues. Thus, for example, we are told that "he will rule . . . with a rod of iron," and that it is he who "will tread the wine press of the fury of the wrath of God."

To all this is now added the description of his clothes as sprinkled or dipped in blood—although we are not told if it is the blood of the Lamb, of the martyrs, or of his enemies. His name is "The Word of God." (Remember that in the first chapter of John's Gospel we are told that Jesus is the Word of God made flesh.) And he has an inscription that proclaims his power: "King of kings and Lord of lords."

Judge: As we saw almost at the beginning of our study of Revelation, the way this book describes Jesus Christ is very different from the pictures that one sees in many churches. In most of those pictures he is calm and even passive with the distant look of a dreamer and with an affable smile. Here we see him as powerful, victorious, and even avenging. After all you have learned about the situation of the believers who first read Revelation, do you understand why this book stresses such a picture of Jesus, rather than the one that is commonly found in our churches?

Ask yourself: Why is it that we prefer to speak of the calm and sweet Jesus, rather that of this Jesus whom John describes in Revelation? Could it be that we prefer that Jesus because he seems to require less from us? Could it be that we prefer him because we are not willing to be faithful, and therefore we would rather have a Jesus who does not judge or destroy his enemies?

Act: Pray: Help me, Lord, to see both your face of love and your face of justice, which in truth are the same face. When I lose heart in seeing my many sins and shortcomings, show me your face of love. When I begin to think that my sins are not so serious, show me the face of your justice. But always, I beseech you, show me your face!

Fourth Day: Read Revelation 19:17-19

See: What the angel announces is a great battle. It is for this that the forces of evil are preparing: the beast, the kings of the earth, and all their armies. The battle will be between those forces on one side, and the one that rides the white horse (that is to say, Jesus Christ) and his army on the other.

Although the battle will be difficult, there is no doubt about the outcome. It is for that reason that the angel summons all the birds of the sky, so that they may gorge themselves with the enemy dead. The contrast between this feast that the birds enjoy and the banquet of the wedding of the Lamb is clear. The banquet of the Lamb is a celebration of eternal life, while the birds will devour the dead bodies of the enemies of the Lord.

It is often said that this battle is the battle of *Harmagadon,* joining what is said here with Revelation 16:16—the only place in the whole Bible where the name *Harmagedon* appears. But in fact there is no reason to join or identify the two. In Revelation there are several visions of battles and conflicts. The only reason people join these two is their desire to put everything in order, thus turning Revelation into a cryptic program for the last days.

Judge: The visions of Revelation are frequently used to inspire terror. Yet the purpose of the book is just the opposite. The angel even announces the victory before it takes place. The victory is assured. Its result is never in doubt.

What may still be in doubt is the side that those who read and hear the book will take. There is no question as to who will win. Now the question to each listener is: When the moment arrives of dividing the forces of the two armies, some to one side, some to the other, where will you be? For those who respond in faith to that question, Revelation has no reason to cause fear. On the contrary, the book assures them that they will conquer.

If, on the other hand, the book causes fear, that may possibly mean that our commitment to Jesus Christ is not completely assured, that we do not want the moment of his victory to arrive because his victory may well be our defeat.

The angel announces the victory before the great battle. You can already know the victory, and even experience some of it today, by just deciding—and deciding firmly—to serve the King of kings and Lord of lords, and refusing to serve the wrong no matter in what appealing form it may be presented to you.

Act: Examine your actions and decisions during the last week. Have you behaved as a person committed to the King of kings? Have you given witness to him, not only with your words but also with your love, and with the justice and rightness of your actions? In such a case, give him thanks for the great victory that is announced.

If, on the other hand, your obedience and your testimony have been not what they should, ask the Lord of lords to forgive you and to strengthen you so that you may be among his true followers and resist the powers of evil.

Fifth Day: Read Revelation 19:20-21

See: The great battle finally takes place. The beast and the false prophet are tossed into a lake of fire that burns with sulfur. On who or what the "false prophet" is, there has been much discussion and no clear answer. He has appeared only once before in the whole book (16:13) and already there John apparently expected his readers to know to what this refers. In any event, it is clear that the "false prophet" is the main agent, the right hand, of the beast, and that as such he is condemned jointly with it.

As for "the rest"—that is, all the armies of those who refused to serve the King of kings and took the mark of the beast—they all die in the great battle. As the angel had announced, "The birds were gorged with their flesh." Notice, however, an important detail. Although great armies surround the Word of God, mounted on a white horse, they are not the ones who kill the enemies. What kills them is "the sword of the rider on the horse, the sword that came from his mouth"—that is to say, the Word of God. In the final battle, it is the Word of God, not the angels or the host of believers that destroys the armies of wickedness.

Judge: Much too often, Christians have taken upon themselves the task of destroying the enemies of the Lord. Thus, crusades were launched against the "unbelievers" and the "heathen." With a similar aim, the Inquisition was organized in order to hunt and to punish those who did not believe exactly as the rest of the church believed. It is so even today, when there are groups and coalitions of Christians whose purpose is to hunt infidels and sinners, to punish them and to destroy them in the name of the Lord.

But this passage seems to indicate that it is not up to us to do such a thing. The destruction of unbelievers and sinners is not our task but rather a task best left to the Word of God—Jesus Christ.

The Word of God, by whom all the things were made and without whom nothing was made, that Word will undo whatever has to be undone. Our function is not to help God in the destruction of God's enemies, but simply to be faithful.

Act: Up to this point, we have repeatedly pleaded for forgiveness from the Lord for the times that we have not been faithful. Now ask for forgiveness for the times you have wanted to destroy or to stop the enemies of God, as if everything depended on you. Notice and admit that this is due to a lack of faith. When Christians think it is up to them to retaliate and to defend the name of the Lord, what that indicates is that we do not have the necessary faith to allow the Lord to attain the victory according to God's own desires and in God's own time. Ask God to give you that faith so you can live a life of joy and of trust even amid so many signs of wickedness.

Sixth Day: Read Revelation 20:1-3

See: The great battle is followed by what would seem to be the final victory of God. The beast and the false prophet have been thrown into the lake of fire and sulfur. The dragon, Satan himself, is chained and locked in the abyss by an angel.

But, to our great astonishment, we are told that this will last only a thousand years, and that after this "he must be let out for a little while."

These thousand years, generally known as the "millennium," have been the subject of bitter controversies among Christians. Some people say that there will be a thousand years of peace after the coming of the Lord and that during those thousand years of peace he will reign over the nations, but that later the Devil will be unchained once again. Others say that the millennium began with the first coming of Christ and will be completed upon his return. Besides these, are many other interpretations.

Unfortunately, in trying to discover what those thousand years are and when they must come, believers have rejected and condemned each other as "premillennialists," "postmillennialists," "amillennialists," and a thousand other groups. Meanwhile, the world looks at Christians with perplexity, and unbelief continues, partly because the witness of the church is obscured and loses its power amid such controversies.

Once again, all this discord is due to attempt to read Revelation as one reads a television program, to see what comes next. But as we have seen repeatedly, Revelation is not a program for the end of the world, but a call to obedience while we wait for the end to arrive.

Judge: John writes his book to brothers and sisters besieged by the persecution. He exhorts them to remain firm. But there is also another serious danger: that things will improve, persecution will end, and the church will begin to imagine that it has already finished its struggle. This has happened many times in the history of the church. There is the danger that this may happen to many of our churches precisely because they are accepted and respected in our society. There is the danger that it may happen to some minority congregations that had difficult struggles in the past but are now being increasingly recognized in society.

Amid those apparently favorable conditions, what we are told in this passage is that, even after the great battle has been won, the struggle does not end. It is necessary to remain alert. The peace and tranquility of the church, even in places where they seem to last a thousand years, will come to an end. When that happens, will we be ready?

Act: During these weeks we have thought repeatedly of the ways in which the beast is manifested in our society and how we must respond. But consider now another subtler temptation: the temptation when things go well to imagine that the struggle has already ended. Maybe in your life Satan is chained. But do not fall asleep. That situation can change. When it does, you have to be ready to face new challenges and temptations. Ask God that, even amid the good times, you be constantly reminded to be alert and prepared against the wiles of the Evil One.

Seventh Day: Read Revelation 20:4-6

See: We continue with some of the most difficult passages in Revelation, again dealing with the theme of the thousand years. But now it gets even more complicated with the introduction of a "first resurrection," in contrast to another that we will see next week (Revelation 20:12-13). Based on this passage, some people say that John announces a resurrection of the bodies of the dead in two stages: first believers, and then the rest of humankind.

But notice that what rises in this "first resurrection" is only "the souls" of the faithful (verse 4). Nothing is said here of the bodies of the dead arising. What is said is that the faithful, although they have died physically, continue living even before the final resurrection. The faithful do not cease existing while waiting for the general resurrection. Rather, they already reign with Christ, and they will continue reigning with him, even before the earth and the sea return their dead, until the day of the final resurrection. Over such people, the "second death"—eternal damnation—has no power.

Judge: Some of the most popular programs for the end of the world are based on this passage and on the rest of this chapter of Revelation. As we saw yesterday, the result has been a series of disputes that have brought little benefit, and many doubts and divisions. Read the passage, not as a chronology of the last times, but as a call to obedience and a word of encouragement in the face of difficulties.

When we read it in that way, the passage says that those who are faithful to the Lord do not have to fear. Certainly they do not have to fear the second death, because they know that they will not be condemned. Nor do they have to fear the first one, because they know that their souls belong to the Lord and that even before the judgment and the final victory they already reign and are royal priests with him. (Notice once again the topic of believers as a royal priesthood that we have found repeatedly in our study [Revelation 1:6; 5:10]; see also 1 Peter 2:9.)

Act: Pray: Thank you, our God, that although we are not able nor should we seek to understand all your mysteries, there is one point at which you assure us: That in you we have and we will have life; that in you we do not have to fear death or any other enemy; that in you we are a royal priesthood; that in you we have victory, peace, security, life. Thank you, Lord. Amen.

For Group Study

Instead of centering your attention only on today's passage, review with the group what we have seen during the whole week. Remind them especially that the victory is ours, not because we have to defeat the enemies, but because they will be defeated by the Lord.

In particular, ask the group to reflect on what difference it might make to believe that the victory depends on us, or to believe that the victory is already assured, and it is the Lord who will conquer. Does the conviction that the victory is the Lord's make it easier for us to love and to forgive our enemies? Does it help us live lives of joy, trusting in the Lord? Does it liberate us from the necessity of attacking evil constantly, from trying to discover who has not been completely faithful, from judging others?

Or pose the question otherwise: When believers act as if the victory over evil depended only on them, are they showing that in fact they do not trust the promise of the Lord's final victory?

W E E K

TWELVE

First Day: Read Revelation 20:7-10

See: The theme of the thousand years continues. But now those thousand years come to their end, and once again a great battle is brewing. The dragon or Satan is now free to carry forth his evil deeds, which consist mainly in deceit. Now his work extends to all the nations—"the nations at the four corners of the earth."

At this point we come to the puzzling reference to "Gog and Magog." According to Genesis and Chronicles, Magog was one of the sons of Japheth, and Gog one of Joel's (Genesis 10:2; 1 Chronicles 1:5; 5:4). As in other cases, their names were also given to their descendants, and therefore Gog and Magog were also names of nations. Both appear repeatedly in Ezekiel 38 and 39, and in some of the later Jewish literature that is not part of the Bible. By then the names of Gog and Magog were used as synonyms for distant peoples. Thus, to say that Satan brings Gog and Magog with himself is another way of saying that even the most distant peoples are prey to his deceit.

All these rise against "the camp of the saints and the beloved city," and they besiege it. But, seemingly without even waiting for the saints to march to battle, God sends fire from heaven and destroys them.

It is now that finally the Devil or dragon is thrown into the lake of fire and sulfur, where we have been told that the beast and the false prophet already are. This punishment will be constant and eternal—"day and night forever and ever."

Judge: Once again, although the victory belongs to God and to the saints, the latter actually do not take part in the battle. They have fought earlier. They are not neutral spectators. On the contrary, Revelation makes it very clear that in the battle between God and the dragon there is no possible neutrality. But although the saints are not neutral, they are not the ones in charge of the battle. Their battle, as we have seen repeatedly, is one of being faithful here on earth. It is a battle against temptation. It is a battle of resistance against the dragon and its minions. But it is not a battle to destroy the enemy. That task is left to God.

Act: If you are following this study as part of a group, review what was said yesterday about the importance of knowing that the victory does not depend on us. Write down what you remember. Meditate on it. Write down your further reflections.

If your study is private, without a group that follows the same study, read yesterday's section "For Group Study." Consider the issues posed there. Write down your reflections.

Second Day: Read Revelation 20:11-15

See: Here the final judgment is depicted. As elsewhere in Revelation, the one who is seated on the throne is God. The throne is white, the color of victory (remember the white horse, the white vestments, and so on).

The image according to which earth and heaven flee is like the pulling back of great curtains. The throne of God is beyond both heaven and earth. Before the presence of God, even heaven flees. The vision is not described in a logical order. First we are told that the dead were standing before God, and then that the sea gave up its dead. What is indicated in any event is a general resurrection from which no one is excluded—even those who were buried at sea. All the dead appear before the celestial throne.

There they are judged according to what is written on several books. The text does not say what these books are, except that one of them is "the book of life." In any event, all are judged, and those whose names do not appear in the book of life are thrown into the fiery lake, where Death and Hades are also thrown. This is the second death, not only because it is eternal death for the condemned, but also because it is the death of death itself.

Judge: We do not like to think of God as a judge. We prefer to see God as a loving Father, as one who forgives, as one who erases our rebellions in divine grace. And all that is true. But the counterpart of the love of God is God's justice. Precisely because God is holy, and because God wants to love all of creation, at the end God must destroy everything that is not holy, all that is not worthy of the divine presence.

Are you ready for the day when you will present yourself before the Lord—before the holy Lord who requires holiness?

Act: Pray: Lord, you alone are holy. In your love, give me of your holiness, so that in the day of judgment I can appear before you and live eternally in your holy presence. Through Jesus Christ, my Lord, the truly Holy One. Amen.

Third Day: Read Revelation 21:1

See: John speaks here of a new creation. Genesis begins by saying that in the beginning God made "the heavens and the earth." In Revelation 20:11, John tells us that heaven and earth fled from the presence of God and that there was no place for them. But now he adds that there is a new creation, a new heaven and a new earth. And he adds that "the sea was no more."

Why does John say "the sea was no more"? There are many possible explanations, but let us consider one in particular. Remember that John was exiled on an island (Patmos) and that what stood between him and his beloved churches was the sea. For John in exile, the sea is a symbol of isolation, of separation. Thus, to say that the sea no longer will exist is to announce a new creation without separations, without isolations, without exiles.

Judge: If what we await is a new creation in which the seas of separation and alienation will no longer exist, shouldn't we give testimony of that faith by putting aside whatever separates or alienates us from one another?

Think about this. Quite likely there are people in your church whom you dislike. But it is with these people that you hope to be in the kingdom of God. Perhaps there are other churches that you dislike. But with them also you will have to be in the kingdom of God. If you seriously believe in that kingdom, is this not the time to begin to practice and to train for it, crossing the seas of separation that keep you away from others with whom in the end you must share that kingdom?

Act: Make a list of brothers and sisters in the faith from whom you are alienated for whatever reason. Write down the list in your notebook. Resolve to approach those people and to try to cross the gap between you and them. Pray for your relationships with each one of them. During the next few days, every time you manage to come closer to one of them, put a star next to his or her name in your list. Continue praying for them and engaging them, until each name on your list has at least one star.

Fourth Day: Read Revelation 21:2-4

See: What is described in these last two chapters of Revelation is the glorious future of God's new creation. All the scenes of destruction that we have encountered in earlier chapters have no other purpose than to open the way for this new creation.

The center of this new creation is the new Jerusalem that descends from heaven, and that is like a bride for her husband (the Lamb). To understand the impact of this imagery, it is important to remember that when John wrote these lines Jerusalem did not exist. The old Jerusalem had been destroyed, and with it many of the hopes of Israel. Thus, what John promises is a new Jerusalem that will be more than the restoration of the old city that no longer exists. This will be a heavenly Jerusalem—not in the sense that it is floating in the clouds, but in the sense that its origin is from on high.

This new Jerusalem will be above all a sign of the permanent presence of God among the people. It will be the home or tabernacle of God with humankind, and "he will dwell with them as their God; they will be his peoples." That relationship will be so close that God "will wipe every tear from their eyes," as a mother wipes the tears from the eyes of her children.

Judge: As we have seen repeatedly, Revelation is mainly a book not of terror and destruction, but of hope and joy. Its last two chapters speak of a new order, a new creation that is the culmination of the purposes of God, and of the restoration of creation in such a way that everything is in communion with God.

As believers, we must read the entire book in the light of these last two chapters. The most important thing to learn from this book is not that there is a beast or a dragon or a great harlot or seven cups of wrath, but rather there will be a new heaven and a new earth, and a new Jerusalem, where God will dry every tear from our eyes.

Act: Think of the most famous of all the hymns inspired by Revelation: "Holy, holy, holy." If you can, sing it aloud. If not, at least repeat the words slowly. Imagine that you are singing it, not alone in your private place for Bible study, but amid the multitude of the people of God, with angels and archangels, in the heavenly Jerusalem. Remember that this is your destiny, your call, and your promise.

Fifth Day: Read Revelation 21:5-8

See: One could say that these verses are the culminating point and the summary of John's visions. Notice that here it is the one who is seated on the throne—God—who tells John to write. And what he is told to write can be summarized in three points: (1) the victory and the power of God: "It is done! I am the Alpha and the Omega, the beginning and the end." (2) The promise to the faithful, repeating what was said at the end of several of the seven letters: "Those who conquer will inherit these things, and I will be their God and they will be my children." (3) The alternative is condemnation: "But as for the cowardly, the faithless...." In those three points the message of the entire book of Revelation is summarized.

Judge: Of those three points, the first is a given and undeniable fact. It is on the other two that we are offered an alternative. What Revelation says, in brief, is that each of us must choose between points two and three: We can be among those people who claim and follow the promise, or among those other ones, for whom there is judgment and condemnation. The decision is ours.

Act: Pray: Thank you, Lord, for your great victory and your great power. And thank you that, in your infinite love, you allow me to be a participant in that victory and that power. Accept me as your child, and sanctify me, so that I may be ready for your presence in the final day. Amen.

Sixth Day: Read Revelation 21:9-21

See: One of the angels that had the cups of wrath offers to show the new Jerusalem to John. It is interesting to note that it was another of those angels that showed him the vision of the great harlot, who represented Babylon/Rome. What is emphasized here is the contrast between two cities: one is imperial Rome, shown to be similar to old Babylon and described as the harlot drunk with the blood of the martyrs; and the other is the Jerusalem that descends from heaven, the faithful bride of the Lamb.

The city is described with a long list of symbolic details. It is not possible in this brief space to discuss them all. But there are three that stand out.

The first is the great size of the city. Earlier, Rome was spoken of as "Babylon the great" (Revelation 17:5). Undoubtedly Rome was the largest city in the known world. But John tells us that the heavenly city measured twelve thousand *stadia* (fifteen hundred miles) in length as well as in width and even in height. Compared with such a city, Rome was but a village!

The second is the wealth of the city. The city itself is made of gold so pure that it is as glass. Its walls are of jasper. Its foundations are adorned with precious stones. Its twelve gates are twelve pearls. It is a vision of such splendor that once again Rome with its temples and its famous buildings is totally eclipsed.

Last, the third topic that stands out is the number twelve. The city has twelve gates with twelve angels, and in them the names of the twelve tribes of Israel are inscribed. And it has twelve foundations, on which the names of the twelve apostles are inscribed. Remembering that the number twelve is a sign of fullness, what we are being told is that the new Jerusalem is the fulfillment of the promises made to Israel and to the church.

Judge: Compare John's vision of this enormous city with the vision we often have of life eternal. In popular art, but also in the imagination of many believers, eternal life consists of floating in the clouds, each one of us on our own private cloud. But John's vision of a great city suggests that the purpose of God is not that people live apart from one another, each in a private cloud, but rather that people relate to one another in love. Notice that the two images or metaphors most frequently employed in the Bible to speak of the future that God promises refer, not to isolated individuals, but to relationships. Those two images are the kingdom of God and the new Jerusalem. Both entities, a kingdom and a city, are terms of relationships among people. In a word, the eternal life that has been promised is life in community.

If eternal life is life in community, what we must do now as believers is to live as those who seriously await that future. That means that we have to begin to practice now for the life in community that we have been promised.

Act: Go back to the list that you made the third day of this week (when studying Revelation 21:1) of people from whom you are alienated. Revise the list. Update it. Decide once again to improve your relationships with those people. Remember that when relationships improve, both you and they are practicing for life in the new Jerusalem, and at the same time proclaiming your Christian hope.

Seventh Day: Read Revelation 21:22-27

See: The most surprising thing in this new Jerusalem may be the fact that there is no temple in it, but rather its temple is none other than God. In the old Jerusalem, the most important building was the temple. The temple is a sign not only of the presence of God, but also of the distance between humans and God. The temple is necessary because the people do not communicate directly and constantly with God. But in the new Jerusalem, where the relationship with God and with the Lamb is direct, immediate, and constant, there is no longer need for a temple.

Likewise, neither are the sun and the moon necessary, for the very presence of God and of the Lamb suffices to illumine the promised city. In the story of creation in Genesis, God made the sun and the moon to illumine God's creation. But now that is no longer necessary, because what illumines the holy city, more than a star in the sky, is God. It is for that reason that later on we are also told that there will be no night in that city. If its light is the presence of God, and that presence is constant, there is no place for darkness or for night.

We may also be surprised that this city, even as large as it is, is not all that exists in the new order after the victory of God. On the contrary, there are also "nations" and "kings of the earth." But even those nations—which continue existing only because they have been saved—will walk by the light of the great city, and the kings of the earth will bring their glory to it. Remember that in previous chapters, every time that the "kings of the earth" were mentioned, it was in order to say how they had fornicated with the great harlot, being devoted to idolatry, or how even after they turned against the harlot they continued serving the beast. But here now the kings of the earth, as well as the nations, are part of the eternal purposes of God.

The gates of the city never close, because there is no need for it. Indeed, the old cities closed their gates at night to avoid surprise attacks, and by day whenever some enemy was nearby. But this city will no longer have any enemies, and therefore it will not be necessary to close its gates.

Yet the open gates do not mean that any person can enter the great city. On the contrary, "only those who are written in the Lamb's book of life"— that is to say, those who survive the judgment of the nations and are invited to enter into the joy of the Lord—will be able to enter the city. (Here again, the character of Revelation as a book of dreamlike visions leaves us perplexed if we take it too literally. Are there people outside the city? Are not all the saved within the city?)

Judge: Think about what John says, that there is no temple in the holy city. We are surprised by this because we usually think— with good reason—that the most important thing in life is religion. We are convinced that what we must put at the very center of our lives is faith, and that if we were to build a new city, what should be placed at its very center is a church or religious building, as a sign of that faith. But it is not so in the holy city.

Why? Because what the text emphasizes is the immediate presence of God. When God is present in that way, there will no longer be any need for a temple or a special place to meet God.

We may be helped to understand this by what Paul says in 1 Corinthians 13:12 to the effect that now we see and know things as through a mirror, darkly, but then we will see face-to-face. Now we know God, certainly; but we know God at some distance, through religion, prayer, and communal worship. But when we see God face-to-face, when what is perfect comes and what is in part passes away (1 Corinthians 13:10), then we will need no mirror to see God. It is as if the mirror were faith. Faith is necessary while we live in hope, awaiting the day of the full presence of God. But when that day arrives, what will remain is love. Remember how Paul finishes that famous chapter 13 of 1 Corinthians: "Now faith, hope, and love abide, these three; and the greatest of these is love."

In the sacred city—a city of such love that the presence of God and of the Lamb is direct and constant, where God will wipe every tear from their eyes—it is no longer necessary to have a temple. Now love reigns. Now God reigns.

It is important that we understand and remember this, because we sometimes think that religion is more important than love. Through the history of the church, there have been Christians making war against other Christians simply because they did not agree on some point of doctrine. Without going that far, even today the churches are divided, and brothers and sisters fight each other over questions such as what the millennium is, when it will come or whether it will come, and similar things. In such a case, niether is right. Both have abandoned the love that is above all doctrine. Therefore, neither party serves the God of love. And whoever does not serve God, as we have seen throughout our study, serves the dragon and the beast.

Act: Think of other Christians with whom you have some serious disagreement, either personal or doctrinal. Do you truly believe that because of that disagreement God will exclude them from the holy city? Will you run the risk, by insisting on your opinion, on your position, or on your feelings, of being one of those who practice the abomination of hatred and who therefore are not allowed to enter the holy city? Is it not likely that in that city you will have to live side by side with these people whom you now reject? Is it not quite likely that, when we finally see face-to-face, we will discover that we have both erred? In that case, why not be reconciled now, while we await the consummation of our hope? Approach those people with whom you disagree. Try to understand those other churches or systems of doctrine. Show them love.

For Group Study

This whole chapter 21 of Revelation is a beautiful poetic description of Christian hope. Since Revelation was written originally to be read aloud in the churches, give the group the opportunity to hear it in that way. Before the meeting, ask somebody who knows how to read well, with clarity and good emphasis, to be ready to read the whole chapter aloud. When the group meets, ask them to imagine that they are the church of Smyrna (if time permits, review briefly what you studied about that church and its situation). Then ask the group to close their Bibles and try listening to the reading of this chapter as if they had never heard or read it before. Give the person who is prepared to do so the opportunity to read the chapter. Then lead the group in a study and discussion of what it says, and why in the holy city there is no temple. Have the group consider what this means for our faith and for our relationships today with other people.

W E E K
THIRTEEN

First Day: Read Revelation 22:1-2

See: Remember God's promise in 21:6 that God would give water from the spring of the water of life to all who are thirsty. Now this promise is fulfilled. An entire river of the water of life flows from the very throne of God and of the Lamb. In a way, this reminds us the vision of Ezekiel 47:1-12, where the prophet says that he saw a river that flowed from the temple and that everywhere the river went it produced life. It also reminds us of Jesus' offer to the Samaritan woman in John 4:14, of giving her "a spring of water gushing up to eternal life." To understand the power of these images, remember that in dry territories where there is always the threat of drought, as in Palestine and Asia Minor. Water was absolutely necessary for life, and its shortage could mean death.

Amid the street, "on either side of the river," stands the tree of life. If the tree is on both sides, the image this evokes in our mind is that of a river running through the tree and under its trunk, much as the river of Ezekiel's vision ran below the threshold of the temple. Also, do not forget that the "tree of life" appears in Genesis 3:22, where God expelled the first couple from the garden in order to prevent them from eating of the tree of life and living forever as sinners.

Thus the holy city is like the Garden of Eden, with the tree of life in the middle. But it is a city, not a garden. History has not passed in vain. Humankind is no longer two people, but multitudes. There is now a city,—a civilization.

But the most remarkable thing is that the tree that is forbidden in Genesis is promised in Revelation. It is promised because now, thanks to the victory of the Lamb, the evil that was introduced in the garden has been destroyed, and therefore redeemed humanity is now ready for life eternal. And the promise is that the tree will constantly give fruit "each month," so that humankind, feeding on it, may live.

Judge: God does not promise a return to Eden in this passage. That was a simple garden where people did not even wear clothes. What is now promised it is a great city—a city so big that it is difficult even to imagine its dimensions. This means that, even while carrying out the work of redemption, God does not undo all that humankind has done between Eden and the final consummation. In antiquity people thought—possibly correctly—that the most important human creation was the city. (What is more, the word "civilization" itself means the construction of cities.) Revelation has some very strong words against the largest and most powerful city in its time, Rome. But still, what is promised at the end is a new city, even greater than Rome itself.

What this means is that God does not discard or condemn all the achievements of human civilization. When believers imagine that what God wants is that we return to the simple life, that we cease studying nature and inquiring how it works, we err. At the end, God will find the way of redeeming not only people who have served God, but also such human achievements as the city.

Therefore, believers, far from thinking that study and scientific advances are always bad, must rather seek ways to put them at the service of this God who takes us as God's collaborators, and at the end promises us, not just the garden of the beginning, but a city.

Act: Pray: Thank you, God, that besides hearts to love and spirits to adore you, you have given us minds to think and hands to build. Take the work of our hands and the thoughts of our minds and use them according to your divine will. Amen.

Second Day: Read Revelation 22:3-5

See: In these verses not much is said that is new; but what the text repeats is very important. Notice in the first place that God and the Lamb share the same throne. In Revelation Jesus Christ is not inferior to the Father, but rather reigns and acts jointly with the Father.

Notice also that the servants of God and of the Lamb bear the name of God on their foreheads. Remember what we read, when studying the sign of the beast, that at that time slaves were sometimes branded as a sign of possession. Whoever takes the sign of the beast serves and belongs to the beast. Whoever takes the name of God serves and belongs to God.

But there is an important detail. These servants can see God's face. A traditional topic in biblical religion is that whoever sees the face of God will die, because the glory of God is too much for a mere human to withstand. Thus, for instance, Moses could not see the face of God (Exodus 3:6). But now it is given to the saints to see the face of God. This is part of that direct relationship with God that is so important in the future that Revelation promises.

Finally, the text says once again that the redeemed "will reign." We are not told, as in other passages, that they will be a priesthood, because in this vision there is no longer a temple and therefore there is no place or need for priests.

Judge: Seeing the face of God is much more than a matter of satisfying the curiosity of knowing what God looks like; it is an indication of how near God is to the redeemed. Since, under other conditions, seeing the face of God is such a terrible experience that one must fear for his or her life, the fact that now the redeemed see that face means that God is near, that their relationship with God is intimate. Now they can really call God Father, and truly have the experience of being God's beloved children whose tears God will wipe away.

Once again, Revelation, rather than a book of terror, is a book of joy and hope, and it closes with tender expressions of the relationship between God and God's own.

Act: Ask God not to be allowed to see God's face right now, but rather for God to prepare and cleanse you so that you may have the joy of gazing upon the divine face in the holy city. And do not forget that such a petition is also a commitment on your part to live in sanctity, as one who prepares to look upon God face to face.

Third Day: Read Revelation 22:6-7

See: Now follows a series of final testimonies on the truth of the visions that John has described in his book. Before coming to the end of the reading, it was important that all who had heard the reading would know that this was not just one more book, nor was it the result of a feverish imagination but rather an authoritative message from God.

The first of these testimonies is provided by the angel that has guided John in his vision of the holy city. The angel testifies that the words of the book are "trustworthy and true," and that it is the Lord who has sent the angel with them. This message from the Lord that the angel communicates is: "See, I am coming soon! Blessed is the who keeps the words of the prophecy of this book."

Judge: Some people interpret verse 7 as a guarantee that the Lord is about to return, if not today, certainly in a few years. But we must remember that these words have been read for almost two thousand years, during which the faithful have been waiting for the return of the Lord. For the Lord, "soon" does not necessarily mean today or tomorrow or even the day after that. It is simply a promise that he will return. And he will return suddenly and unexpectedly—"like a thief in the night."

Much more important than the date is that we understand our calling to keep "the words of the prophecy of this book." This does not mean to keep the book in a drawer. Nor does it mean to spend time trying to figure out all the mysteries about the last days. It means rather to obey the message of God, the prophecy in the sense of what God tells us and requires of us. (Unfortunately, in common usage a "prophecy" is an announcement of future events. This is not the meaning of the term in the Bible, where a prophet is one who speaks for God and any such speech is a prophecy, whether it refers to the future, the present, or even the past,)

Act: Begin reviewing what you have been studying during these three months. Thumb through your notebook and see what you have written. To what extent have you done what you promised? What can you do to be more faithful and to keep "the words of the prophecy"? Write down the result of this initial review, your conclusions, and any resolutions.

Fourth Day: Read Revelation 22:8-9

See: The testimonials about the authority of the book continue. It was customary at the time for the person writing or dictating a book to close it by affirming that its words were indeed his or hers. In Galatians 6:11, for instance, Paul closes the letter by writing in his own hand. In this case, John says that it was he who saw and heard the things about which he had written. It is as a sort of warranty from the author on behalf of the book that bears his name.

John confesses that he prostrated himself in worship before the angel that had served him as a guide. Such a thing was natural, because this angel had shown extraordinary power and wisdom. But the angel forbids it, insisting that John must worship God alone.

Judge: It may surprise us that John, who has just written such a convincing book about the need to worship God alone, and to neither worship nor serve the beast, is now ready to adore the angel. This is the second time that John comes to the edge of that error. One would imagine that John, who had received so many warnings against idolatry, would know quite well that he must not worship angels, but only God. Yet when he has a startling vision, its impact is such that he bows before the angel, who explains it to him as if the angel were God.

If an angel can tempt John to fall into idolatry, we must be always vigilant against such a temptation. Have you not known cases where the admiration of some parishioners for their pastor seemed to border on worship because the pastor was such an admirable person and spoke for God? This too is idolatry, not service to God.

Act: If you feel tempted to render to some person, program, or institution a loyalty that is due only to God, stop to think about it. Repent. While still admiring that person, or participating in that program or institution, make certain that your faith centers in God. Make sure that, even if that person, program, or institution fail you, your faith will remain strong because it depends not on them, but on God.

If, on the contrary, you fear that some other person offers you an excessive loyalty or admiration, do as the angel that reminded John that he should not worship anything else but God alone.

Fifth Day: Read Revelation 22:10-13

See: It is not clear who speaks here. It would seem to be the angel who continues speaking. But what he says are words that properly can be spoken only by the Lord. Thus, either the Lord is speaking or the angel is quoting the message of the Lord to John and his readers.

John is told not to seal the book that he has just written. The normal thing to do when finishing a document, particularly a letter or a legal document that would be read later, such as a will, was to seal it so that nobody could alter what had been said in the document. But John receives instructions not to seal the book, "for the time is near." This contrasts with the instructions that are given to the prophet Daniel to seal book because the time of its fulfillment has not arrived (Daniel 8:26). Nor is John's book like the one he himself saw, sealed with seven seals that only the Lamb was worthy of opening.

The book must not be sealed because it is a warning and an immediate exhortation to its addressees. John's message is one of immediate validity for the seven churches of the Roman province of Asia, and of continuous validity for the rest of the church through the ages. It is not necessary to seal it until some future event is completed. It is not a message that will have value, as some people think, only when the day of the final judgment comes—or at least the day of the seventh seal. It is an open message for the church of that time and for the church of today. It is not sealed because it has meaning without waiting for future events and without mysterious interpretations.

And the message is indeed clear. Verse 11 repeats it, apparently in an ironic fashion. Let the evildoers continue doing evil without paying attention to the message. Let the filthy continue in their filth, as if it didn't matter. But let the righteous practice justice, and the saints' holiness, because the Lord comes shortly. When he comes, he will repay according to everyone's work—according to how they responded to the warnings of this book.

The passage ends with a reiteration of who the Lord is: "I am the Alpha and the Omega, the first and the last, the beginning and the end."

Judge: Ironically, the book that the angel told John not to seal is the book that appears to be sealed to many readers of the New Testament. This is due to those erroneous interpretations to which I have referred several times in the course of this study—interpretations that make of Revelation a mysterious program for the last events, and that claim that Revelation is a book that only those who know a secret code or key can understand.

But the truth is that Revelation is an open book that says essentially the same as the rest of the New Testament, although in symbolic language: that Jesus Christ, the Lamb that was slaughtered and yet lives, will reign; that those who follow him and are faithful will reign with him; and that those who refuse to follow him, and instead practice injustice and idolatry, will receive eternal punishment.

Act: Write, in not more than three or four sentences, what you understand to be the message of Revelation. Read again some of the passages that have affected you most during this study. See if what you have written is what those passages say. Share your results with others.

Sixth Day: Read Revelation 22:14-15

See: Once again, these two verses summarize the message of Revelation. Verse 14 summarizes what is said of the faithful, and verse 15 what is said of the others.

Washing their robes is, naturally, a way of referring to redemption. In Revelation 7:13 we are told that the great multitude of all the nations that praises the Lord are those who "have washed their robes and made them white in the blood of the Lamb." (This may also be a reference to baptism, for it was customary, when leaving the baptismal waters, to give the believer a white robe as a sign of cleansing and victory.) Only those who have washed their clothes in the blood of the Lamb can enter through the doors of the holy city because "nothing unclean will enter it, nor anyone who practices abomination or falsehood" (Revelation 21:27). And, since the tree of life is at the center of the city, they will be able to eat of it and have eternal life.

On the other hand, those who have not washed their robes will be "outside," and they will not be able to enter. Such people practice a multitude of sins that bar their way into the holy city. They are sorcerers, fornicators, murderers, idolaters, and liars. The reference to "the dogs" that must remain outside may mean one of two things. On the one hand, those "dogs" may be this whole list of sinful people. Thus, for instance, Paul in Philippians 3:2 refers to certain people as "dogs." But it can also mean that those who are outside of the city will be devoured by dogs, because in the Old Testament one of the worst calamities that could befall a person was to be devoured by dogs (for example, in 1 Kings 14:11; 16:4; 21:19).

Judge: The alternatives are clear. The whole book of Revelation has emphasized them. It is necessary to serve either God or the dragon and the beast. It is necessary to be washed in the blood of the Lamb or to remain in filthiness. It is necessary to get ready to enter the holy city or to be left outside of it, among the dogs. After this study, what will you choose?

Act: Since Revelation tells us that it is necessary to take either the mark of the beast or the seal of Jesus Christ, decide which sign you will bear. Write on your notebook, with no other commentary, two things: "666" and "The Lamb of God." You must cross out one of the two. Cross out the 666, and imagine that what now remains on the page is also written on your forehead. At different points during the day, imagine that you actually bear that sign on the forehead and act accordingly.

Seventh Day: Read Revelation 22:16-21

See: We finally come to the last of the words of testimony that conclude the book and warrant its authority. The first testimony came from the angel. The second was John's. But now we come to the highest commendation: "I, Jesus." It is Jesus who endorses the authority of the book with his authority. The message does not come from an angel—not even the highest of all the angels—but from Jesus himself.

The Spirit and the bride then join this testimonial, inviting readers: "Come." And then those who have been invited and who hear this testimony join in it by inviting others: "let everyone who hears say, 'Come'".

But the testimony is not only about the authority of the book. It is also a curse on any who dare change it. Jesus himself warns any who dare add to the book that evil will be added to them ("God will add to that person the plagues described in this book"), and whoever dares to take away from it will be erased from the book of life.

The book closes with the promise of Jesus that he will return to his people, and with the petition that it may be so: "Amen. Come, Lord Jesus!" This is followed by the closing benediction.

The words "Come, Lord Jesus" were frequently pronounced at the beginning of the Lord's Supper. Sunday worship in the early church consisted of two parts: the service of the Word and the service of the Table. In the service of the Word, the Scriptures were read and explained—much as we do today in the sermon. The service of the Table was communion. Remember that this book is being read aloud in the church, probably in place of a sermon. Now, when finishing the reading that would be made during the service of the Word, the church gets ready to celebrate communion and hears the familiar words, "Come, Lord Jesus!" Those words have a double reference. On one hand, they are an expression of the yearning of the church through the centuries that the Lord will come and our longing will be fulfilled. On the other hand, it is a call to Jesus to be present in communion. (Remember your study of the words from Jesus to the church in Laodicea [Revelation 3:20]: "Listen! I am standing at the door, knocking; if you hear my voice and open the door, I will come in to you and eat with you, and you with me.")

Judge: The book of Revelation, precisely because it is a series of visions and uses symbolic language, has been vulnerable to subtraction and to addition. People add to it by wanting the book to tell them more that it actually says. Thus, some read the book to discover when the Lord will come, and interpretations are concocted that claim we are living under this or that particular trumpet, or after this or that particular seal. This is to add to the book, because such it is not the purpose of the book, nor does it tell such things.

In reaction to that kind of interpretation, there are those who simply ignore the book. Since they find it mysterious, they neither study it nor pay any attention to it. Such people subtract from the book.

Between those attitudes, there is another approach—one of serious study and obedience. If we have this attitude, we study the book because it is the Word of God. Precisely because it is God who is speaking, we do not try to solve mysteries that are not for us to know or penetrate.

When we read the book in this way, its message is clear: one must choose between God and the Lamb on one hand, or their enemies on the other. It is not possible to sit on the fence, without deciding. Whoever does not decide is in fact siding against God and the Lamb.

Act: Review what you have written in your notebook during these three months. Review your own life and see in what ways it has changed, and in what ways it still needs to change. Write in your notebook one or two paragraphs that may help you, whenever you find your faith or your obedience vacillating, to reaffirm your decisions of these months.

Finally, do not abandon your discipline of biblical study. Make plans to begin studying another book of the Bible—tomorrow, if at all possible.

For Group Study

Ask the group to make a list of the things that have had the most impact on them during these three months of study. Write what they say on newsprint or on a blackboard. Use that list for a review of the message of the book.

Finish the session by inviting the group to undertake the study of another book of the Bible. Come to an agreement on the topic and make the commitment to continue with a discipline of study.

Finally, thank you, my brothers and my sisters, for this opportunity of studying the Word of God with you. May the Lamb who was slaughtered bless you and keep you. Come, Lord Jesus! Amen!